People Power?

People Power?

The Role of the Voluntary and Community Sector in the Northern Ireland Conflict

Feargal Cochrane
and
Seamus Dunn

CORK UNIVERSITY PRESS

First published in 2002 by
Cork University Press
Crawford Business Park
Crosses Green
Cork
Ireland

British Library Cataloguing in Publication Data
A CIP catalogue record for this book is available from the British Library.

Library of Congress Cataloguing-in-Publication Data
Cochrane, Feargal
People Power?: the role of the voluntary and community sector in the Northern Ireland conflict / Feargal Cochrane and Seamus Dunn.
p. cm.
Includes bibliographical references and index.
ISBN 1-85918-302-6 (alk. paper)
1. Conflict management – Northern Ireland. 2. Peace movements – Northern Ireland. 3. Nonprofit organizations – Northern Ireland. 4. Community organization – Northern Ireland. 5. Voluntarism – Northern Ireland. 6. Volunteer workers in community development – Northern Ireland. I. Dunn, Seamus, 1930– II. Title.

HN398.N6 C63 2002
303.6'9'09416–dc21

2001037289

ISBN 1 85918 302 6 (HB)

Typeset by Mark Heslington, Scarborough, North Yorkshire
Printed by MPG Books Ltd, Cornwall

Contents

Abbreviations

APNI	Alliance Party of Northern Ireland
CCRU	Central Community Relations Unit
CVRDC	Clogher Valley Rural Development Centre
CAJ	Committee on the Administration of Justice
CRC	Community Relations Council
DHRC	Dove House Resource Centre
FAIT	Families Against Intimidation and Terror
NUS/USI	National Union of Students/Union of Students in Ireland
NIVT	Northern Ireland Voluntary Trust
NIWC	Northern Ireland Women's Coalition
PP	Peace People
PT	Peace Train
PUP	Progressive Unionist Party
QH	Quaker House
SDLP	Social Democratic and Labour Party
SICDP	Springfield Inter-Community Development Project
T&EA	Training and Employment Agency
UCAN (Londonderry)	Ulster Community Action Network
UDA	Ulster Defense Assoiciation
UDP	Ulster Democratic Party
UPC	Ulster People's College
UUC	Ulster Unionist Council
UUP	Ulster Unionist Party
WT	Women Together for Peace

You coasted along
To larger houses, gadgets, more machines,
To golf and weekend bungalows,
Caravans when the children were small,
The Mediterranean, later, with the wife.

. . . You showed a sense of responsibility,
with subscriptions to worthwhile causes
and service in voluntary organizations;
and, anyhow, this did the business no harm,
no harm at all.
Relations were improving. A good
Useful life. You coasted along.

. . . Now the fever is high and raging;
who would have guessed it, coasting along?
The ignorant-sick thresh about in delirium
And tear at the scabs with dirty fingernails.
The cloud of infection hangs over the city,
A quick change of wind and it
might spill over the leafy suburbs.
You coasted too long.

John Hewitt[1]

[1] John Hewitt, *The Coasters*, in F. Ormsby (ed.), *A Rage for Order: Poetry of the Northern Ireland Troubles* (Belfast: Blackstaff Press, 1992), pp. 49–51.

Preface

This book is the result of a three-year project studying the evolution and impact of non-governmental peace/conflict resolution organizations in Northern Ireland. The research was funded by the Aspen Institute in Washington DC, as part of the International Study of Peace Organizations (ISPO) project. This brought together researchers in Northern Ireland, South Africa and Israel/Palestine to examine the development of such NGOs in these four areas of emerging peace processes. The authors were responsible for the Northern Ireland element of this project.

The last thirty years of conflict in Northern Ireland have witnessed the emergence of a vast range of initiatives and groups who have worked energetically to reduce violence and promote reconciliation within the community. These have varied enormously in size, function and philosophy from ad hoc non-formalized and unfunded groupings with no paid employees, through to large, formal, state-funded agencies with six-figure annual budgets and a professional salaried workforce. These individuals and organizations have worked tirelessly over many years to promote peace and reconciliation, while others have taken a more oblique approach to conflict resolution by seeking to regenerate the 'marginalized' and 'socially excluded' via community development initiatives. Much of this work has taken place against the backdrop of vicious and internecine community conflict and has paralleled the political process that led eventually to the Good Friday Agreement of April 1998.

Despite the work that has taken place, however, very little is known about these peace/conflict resolution organizations (P/CROs) or about their contribution to the social and political fabric of Northern Ireland. While opinions of the 'peace sector' may exist, these are based more often upon subjective perspectives than empirical evidence. There is a general understanding that 'peace groups' have been active within Northern Ireland for the last thirty years, and have been campaigning against intimidation and violence. Many people would be aware of organizations such as the Peace People and their public protests in the 1970s, but would perhaps be less au fait with the range and complexity of the sector as a whole. While some would take the view that these P/CROs are 'a good thing' and applaud them for their efforts (however ineffective), others speak more critically of the 'community relations industry' and see the activities of P/CRO groups as being irrelevant within the political process. This view frequently contends that such work is born of a misunderstanding as to how politics (and the politics of conflict) work in Northern Ireland, and is more often cited by those who possess a structural rather than behavioural analysis of the political situation. Such critics tend to place the emphasis upon the 'peace' rather than the 'conflict resolution' aspects of P/CRO activity, and suggest disdainfully that much of this work is engaged in by well-meaning though muddle-headed peaceniks, or the 'great and the good' looking for philanthropic projects to keep themselves busy between appointments at the golf club! This extremely negative view of the P/CRO sector is at the opposite end of the scale to those who are simply glad that such groups exist, however nebulous the effects of their work. Both of these extreme positions are based on an incomplete knowledge of the diversity of organizations that exist, the work that is carried out, or the impact that it has upon the political process.

For understandable reasons, the spotlight has focused on track-one diplomacy and the efforts of political élites to construct and implement a settlement. It is the political leaders and paramilitary factions within Northern Ireland, together with external actors within the British, Irish and American administrations, who have had the most immediate effect upon the political process. There is a danger here, however, of buying into a simplified media-driven view, where politics is seen as a minority sport presided over by half a dozen middle-class men. In reality of course, the political and social dynamics that shape a society's evolution are not held within a hermetically sealed world where grey men in grey suits argue over policy documents. Within the context of Northern Ireland this should not be surprising, given that over 50 per cent of the population is female.

While these political and factional élites have been important in Northern Ireland, both in perpetuating the conflict and in constructing the 'peace process', politics is about much more than this track-one level, reaching right down through society in the form of track-two interventions by special interest groups and community organizations, within what is often referred to as the 'third sector', or alternatively, 'civil society'. As this book will demonstrate, such language is itself part of the debate, with some buying into phrases such as 'community relations', 'inclusive dialogue' and 'civil society', while others regard them as the trite utterances of the liberal middle classes. As one commentator has said in relation to the last of these terms,

> we are dealing with a concept which is interesting, which promises to help us understand some important aspects of reality, yet which is vague, stretched, contested. For some, civil society may be strong in a place where there is great diffusion and little civility, but strong representation through 'pressure groups' and 'non-governmental organizations', whereas for others it is more important to have civility and *Gemeinschaft* associations which work by habit and assumption.[2]

This book seeks to shed some light on this sector by focusing on organizations within this civil society that have a particular interest in peace/conflict resolution, and examining their role during the conflict and subsequent peace process. What types of organizations are involved? Who participates in this sort of activity? How do such groups understand and seek to address the conflict in Northern Ireland? Where do these P/CROs get their resources from to carry out their programmes and activities? Most importantly perhaps, given the amount of work that has been done by these organizations, not to mention the amount of money that has been channelled into them, the book will assess the impact of the P/CRO sector and the contribution that these groups have made to progressive political and social change in Northern Ireland.

It will become clear in the forthcoming chapters, that these organizations are complex in their evolution, structure, ideological focus and goals. We hope that this book highlights that complexity and

[2] L. Allison, 'Sport and Civil Society', *Political Studies*, vol. 46, no. 4., September 1998, p. 713.

adds to public understanding of the P/CRO sector, together with the society within which they operate.

This book would not have been written without the support and guidance of the Aspen Institute who funded the original ISPO project within which most of the research was conducted. The authors also benefited hugely from the assistance provided by a steering group of academics and NGO practitioners, together with the leadership of the project directors, Professor Benjamin Gidron, Ben Gurion University, Israel, and Professor Stan Katz, Princeton University, USA. We would like to thank the following members of the Steering Group for the useful advice they provided over the last three years: Professor Adrian Guelke, Queen's University, Belfast; Mr Quintin Oliver, former director of the Northern Ireland Council for Voluntary Action (NICVA) and currently director of the Stratagem lobbying group; Professor Ed Cairns, University of Ulster, Coleraine; Dr Deirdre Heenan, University of Ulster, Coleraine; Professor Sally McClean, University of Ulster, Coleraine.

The International Advisory Board and the other research team members within the ISPO study also provided the authors with fresh insights and perspectives and we would like to thank the following people for their valuable contributions: Mr Alan Abramson; Professor Helmut Anheier; Professor Galia Golan; Dr Adam Habib; Professor Manuel Hassassian; Professor Tamar Hermann; Dr Virginia Hodgkinson; Professor Wilmot James; Dr Dirk Rumberg; Dr Rupert Taylor .

The authors are also thankful for the guidance and insights provided by an Advisory Committee that was established at the beginning of the study and we would like to thank the following members for their assistance: Mr Gerry Burns, Parliamentary Ombudsman; Ms Evelyn Collins, formerly of the Equal Opportunities Commission; Ms Joan Harbinson, Race Relations Commission; Mr Paul Sweeney, formerly of the District Partnership Board; and Ms Maeve Walls, formerly of the Citizen's Advice Bureaux.

The research on which this book is based was carried out by the authors within the Centre for the Study of Conflict, at the University of Ulster in Coleraine. We would like to thank all of the people we worked with at the Centre for their help and support, particularly, Helen Dawson, Gregory Irwin, Alison Montgomery, Valerie Morgan, Ruth McIlwaine and Pat Shortt. Feargal Cochrane would also like to thank his colleagues within the Department of Politics and International Relations at Lancaster University, especially Gordon Hands and Hugh Miall.

The last word must go to the groups themselves and the many individuals within the NGO sector who participated in the project and who are too numerous to mention individually. Their willingness to discuss the history, evolution and perspectives of their organizations and give up precious time to the research was invaluable and is much appreciated by the authors.

Feargal Cochrane
Seamus Dunn
November 2001

1
Introduction

Northern Ireland P/CROs in comparative perspective

> NGOs at best embody values of liberalism and democracy, unsullied by more Machiavellian considerations to which governments are prone, which are indispensable ingredients of a civil society. They also have deep concrete experience to bring to bear of the struggle to maintain such civilities in the face of centrifugal forces of conflict.[1]

> Clearly, it is quite unsustainable to suggest that the needs of the most disadvantaged can be met by the voluntary sector. Civil society based purely on the principle of private altruism would not be a civilised society. Indeed, there is no essential link between civil society and a civilised society – contrary to Paine's view. Civil Society has a chequered political history. The Nazi party undermined the Weimar Republic in Germany by infiltrating local organisations. It should not be forgotten that the Mafia is an intermediate institution.[2]

For the past two decades, non-governmental organizations (NGOs) have played an increasingly prominent role in progressive social change throughout the world. In 1997, the Carnegie Commission on Preventing Deadly Conflict recognized this developing role and identified three general categories of NGO participation in the process of conflict resolution, namely: human rights and advocacy groups, humanitarian and service organizations, and mediation groups that may act as intermediaries between the formal negotiating process and the wider community. The report identifies the ways in which this disparate collection of organizations can make a positive contribution to peace processes as they have the ability to:

> monitor conflicts and provide early warnings and insight into a particular conflict; convene the adversarial parties (provide a neutral forum);

1 *New Order? International Models of Peace and Reconciliation*, Democratic Dialogue, 1st edn, Report No. 9, May 1998, Belfast, p. 9.

2 F. Powell and Donal Guerin, *Civil Society and Social Policy* (Dublin: A&A Farmar, 1997), p. 24.

> pave the way for mediation and undertake mediation; carry out education and training for conflict resolution, building indigenous capacity for coping with ongoing conflict; help to strengthen institutions for conflict resolution; [and] foster the development of the rule of law.[3]

In three recent centres of political conflict, Northern Ireland, South Africa and Israel/Palestine, a diverse array of peace/conflict resolution organizations (P/CROs) were involved to some degree within the political process prior to, during and after the establishment of major peace agreements and ceasefires. To date, the academic literature on these conflicts has concentrated on the élite-level, track-one diplomacy and the struggle between the parties, with little attention being given to the equally important community-based track-two initiatives that are essential to building and sustaining peace processes.

The parameters of what constitutes a peace/conflict resolution group are defined here in a very broad sense to include community development groups and those that would see their primary focus falling within social and economic issues. While being a complex grouping in themselves, P/CROs, in this context, clearly fall within that category loosely referred to as NGOs, or the Third Sector as outlined by Salamon and Anheier (1996).[4]

[3] Carnegie Commission on Preventing Deadly Conflict (1997), *Preventing Deadly Conflict: Final Report*, p. 4 in B. Gidron, S. Katz, M. Meyer, Y. Hasenfeld, R. Schwartz and J. Crane, 'Peace and Conflict Resolution Organizations in Three Protracted Conflicts: Structures, Resources and Ideology', *Voluntas: International Journal of Voluntary and Non-Profit Organisations*, vol. 10, no. 4, 1999, pp. 276–7.

[4] See L. Salamon and H. Anheier, *The Emerging Non-Profit Sector: An Overview*, (Manchester University Press, 1996). The authors define the parameters of the sector, mindful of the pitfalls associated with the variable terminologies of the American 'non-profit sector', or European 'voluntary sector'. However, they provide a useful summary of the boundaries that set the limits for what will be referred to in this book as non-governmental organizations, with peace/conflict resolution organizations being a branch thereof: 'The non-profit sector embraces a vast collection of organizations that share five common features. They are: (a) formally constituted; (b) organizationally separate from government; (c) non-profit-seeking; (d) self-governing; and (e) voluntary to some significant degree.' (pp. xvii–xviii). See also Thomas G. Weiss (1996), who defines the use of the term NGO succinctly 'it is widely accepted (following the language of Article 71 of the UN Charter) and because "non-state actors" include a host of transnational entities that should be deliberately excluded from this discussion, such as profit-making corporations, political parties, religious groups,

Politics generally, and conflict resolution in particular, is too often analysed at the élite level, with little emphasis being given to the communities from whom the élite political actors derive their authority. In fact, as this book will demonstrate, those communities play an important role in developing peace processes within divided societies. One important manifestation of this 'grass roots' level is the P/CRO sector and the multitude of NGOs from which it derives.

From a wider comparative perspective, the ending of the cold war and the increasing frequency with which the international community has intervened in intra-state and ethno-nationalist conflicts and mediated within the sovereign borders of war-torn societies, has meant that NGOs have increasingly found themselves in a more central position vis-à-vis third party interventions. Thomas Weiss makes the case well when referring to the importance of NGOs in conflict resolution activity: 'Because they provide assistance and protect the rights of civilians caught in the throes of internal conflicts, they are worthy of analytical attention.'[5] The purpose of this book is to provide that analytical attention for the NGOs that have been active within Northern Ireland and have sought to engage in peace and conflict resolution activity.

Much has been written about the track-one level of diplomacy involved in the political negotiations that led ultimately to peace 'agreements' in all of these cases,[6] yet relatively little attention has been paid to track-two involvement, namely, the lower-profile activities of community workers and local conflict-resolution organizations within these divided societies. The book will examine the work of the

banks, criminal organizations, terrorists, insurgents, and the media' (op. cit.), pp. 436–7.

5 Thomas G. Weiss, 'Non-governmental Organisations and Internal Conflict', in Michael E. Brown (ed.), *The International Dimensions of Internal Conflict.* (Cambridge, MA: MIT Press, 1996), p. 437.

6 See, for example, M. Abbas, *Through Secret Channels.* (Reading: Garnet Publishing, 1995) and J. Corbin, *Gaza first: The Secret Norway Channel to Peace between Israel and the PLO* (London: Bloomsbury, 1994) for records of the negotiations leading to the signing of the Oslo Accord. E. Mallie and D. McKittrick, *The Fight for Peace: The Secret Story behind the Peace Process* (Belfast: Blackstaff Press, 1997); M. Cox, A. Guelke and F. Stephen (eds.), *A Farewell to Arms: From 'long war' to 'long peace' in Northern Ireland* (Manchester University Press, 2000); P. Gastrow, *Bargaining for Peace: South Africa and the National Peace Accord* (Washington, DC: United States Institute for Peace, 1995).

NGO sector and the wider civil society[7] within which it is located, to determine its role and significance within the peace process in Northern Ireland.

It is important to recognize that the culture of the track-one negotiations that led ultimately to negotiated agreements in Northern Ireland (and in other divided societies such as South Africa and Israel/Palestine), was significantly different from the ethos held at the track-two level of civil society. While political compromises were made by all of the negotiating parties within the three regions, these were essentially bargained trade-offs between the élite representatives of conflict parties, rather than an achievement of mutual consensus on the issues underlying the respective conflicts. Consequently, the post-settlement period has been characterized by stalemate and inertia due to the continuation of conflict within the political sphere. In Northern Ireland, for example, the inability of this 'historic compromise' to translate into a *transformation* of the political conflict following the Good Friday Agreement in April 1998, was highlighted during the subsequent referendum campaign. Here, nationalists and unionists who had 'compromised', campaigned separately rather than together, and in the case of Sinn Féin and the Ulster Unionist Party, gave their respective supporters opposite messages with regard to the meaning of the agreement they had signed. While UUP leader David Trimble claimed that it secured Northern Ireland's position within the Union, Sinn Féin President Gerry Adams was arguing that it was a transitional step towards Irish unity. From this perspective, the Good Friday Agreement of April 1998 can be seen as being the product of a tug-of-war between the track-one negotiators rather than any transformation in their ideological positions or any paradigm-

[7] This too can be an elastic concept and is sometimes stretched to the point that it becomes meaningless. It is used here to refer to the groups, associations, and individuals from trade unions, churches, business communities, educational sectors, media and the arts, NGOs and pressure groups etc. that mediate between the individual and the state. The term is used in conjunction with its common usage, to mean those non-governmental individuals and groups that make a positive engagement with the liberal-democratic polity. It is understood that some groups that could be categorized as falling within the definition of 'civil society' (e.g. the Chinese Triads, Los Angeles street gangs or Northern Ireland paramilitary organizations) are anything but civil and they would be excluded from this definition of the term as employed here. A recent study of civil society in Ireland makes this point well.

shift in the underlying dynamics of the political conflict. In fact, it was only when civil society activists became mobilized in the form of the independent 'Yes' campaign during the referendum, that a consistent message was given to the Northern Ireland electorate, which allowed the political class to focus on the inclusive and progressive aspects of the Agreement.

The emphasis at the track-two level therefore, as this book will demonstrate, tended to be *process*-driven rather than *outcome*-driven, with the majority of P/CROs being immersed more thoroughly in a consensus-building exercise rather than in engineering a particular 'solution' or hammering out a political deal. This culture, which emphasized inclusiveness and dialogue, eventually filtered up into the track-one level negotiations and made a positive contribution to the political process. This was personified by the creation of the Northern Ireland Women's Coalition (NIWC) in 1996, a party drawn substantially from the NGO sector that took a consensus-building approach to the nationalist/unionist ideological divide in the negotiations that led to the Good Friday Agreement in April 1998.

The book will argue that while the contribution of the P/CRO sector was not crucial to the eventual outcome of the political negotiations in 1998, it was nonetheless positive and significant.

Peace and conflict resolution in comparative perspective

It is not possible to generalize about the nature of P/CROs without understanding that their ideology and activities are heavily influenced by the environment within which they try to operate. As a consequence, understandings and definitions of what is meant by terms such as 'peace' or 'conflict resolution' vary widely, depending on the specific regional context, the nature of the political conflict, and the state of the 'peace process'. A comparison of the roles of peace/conflict resolution organizations within a number of separate regional contexts, namely South Africa, Northern Ireland, and Israel/Palestine,[8] illustrates the point. An examination of the context

[8] This comparison is based on the evidence from research carried out by the South African, Northern Ireland, Israeli and Palestinian research teams who participated in the International Study of Peace and Reconciliation Organisations.

and structure of these conflicts quickly illustrates that, while the terminology of 'peace' and 'conflict resolution' that is used may be the same, its meaning and significance can vary substantially.

The following comment from Rupert Taylor indicates that in the case of South Africa, P/CROs (together with the wider civil society within which such groups were located) had a cohesive political project, which was aimed at reforming the apartheid system of government:

> Amongst the social forces that made for peace, for creating the 'new' South Africa, were the innovative actions of an ever-increasing network of progressive movements, institutions, non-governmental organizations, and associations (which included churches, trade unions, civics, and women's groups) engaged in a 'war of position' against apartheid rule and mainly aligned to the African National Congress. This network of anti-apartheid organizations created an alternative space outside distorted and limited binary racial thinking, seeking to undercut the apartheid state's reification of 'race' and 'ethnicity', and promote the idea of a common society.[9]

With regard to South Africa therefore, the P/CRO profile is relatively clear and coherent. They all shared the same fundamental goal, namely, they all organized around their opposition to apartheid and they all espoused a 'positive view' of peace. This defined 'peace' as being not simply the absence of physical violence, but the creation of social and political conditions such as justice and equality that would allow real peace to emerge. The majority of P/CROs active in South Africa during the apartheid years were not 'neutral', in that they shared a common commitment (although expressed differently) to the abolition of apartheid and the establishment of at least some form of democratic, non-racial society.[10] Most of the NGOs in South Africa with a conflict-resolution focus simply used a variety of different methods and engaged in different activities to achieve these goals. In ideological terms therefore, peace/conflict resolution organ-

[9] R. Taylor, 'Northern Ireland: Consociation or Social Transformation?', in J. McGarry (ed.), *Northern Ireland and the Divided World* (Oxford: Oxford University Press, 2001, p. 41).

[10] R. Taylor, A. Egan, A. Habib, J. Cock, A. Lekwane and M. Shaw, Executive Summary: International Study of Peace and Conflict Resolution Organisations – South Africa. Unpublished paper given to the Third International Conference of the International Society for Third Sector Research (ISTR), Geneva, 8–12 July 1998, p. 2.

izations in South Africa were not 'pacifist'[11] during the apartheid years. The very idea of being a 'peace organization', or a 'non-violent' organization, was a difficult one for South African NGOs who were against the apartheid system, because the government also claimed to be in favour of peace and bringing an end to the conflict.[12] They were in favour of restoring peace through 'order', via harsh anti-democratic legislation and the enforcement of that legislation by a ruthless law and order regime. As a consequence of what many would regard as a warped sense of peace, the NGOs in South Africa had to emphasize a positive (Galtungian) view of peace, as being not simply the restoration of order or a reduction in physical violence, but rather the more positive view, namely the creation of justice and equality for all.[13] Consequently, what South African P/CROs meant by 'peace' and what Israelis or Northern Ireland P/CROs meant, was not necessarily the same. For the South Africans, peace was not simply about ending violence, but was primarily concerned with overturning what they saw as an illegitimate and anti-democratic form of government. South African P/CROs can be regarded as fundamentally different from many of their counterparts in Israel and Northern Ireland, as they had a more developed sense of political direction. They were all committed to bringing apartheid to an end and replacing it with a new political system based on equality and freedom from political and economic oppression.

By contrast, the P/CRO sector in Northern Ireland is much more diverse. It does not have the same coherent political goals as its counterpart had in South Africa. They are not all on the same side with the one goal of smashing a system like apartheid. Some activists come from the Protestant community, others from the Catholic community, while yet others are based on a cross-community membership and draw support from both sides. While some are driven by a clearly defined sense of political direction, many others are not. While some adopt a general human rights remit, others focus

11 'Pacifist' is used here to mean totally committed to non-violence as the central belief around which the organization was constructed.

12 This is true of most of the protagonists and conflict parties within divided societies, including the Provisional IRA, the British government, the PLO and successive Israeli administrations.

13 See Johan Galtung, *Peace by Peaceful Means* (International Peace Research Institute Oslo (PRIO), 1996).

on a single issue. While some attempt to mobilize public opinion, others shy away from the limelight, preferring to work quietly within their communities.

Clearly then, there is not the same cohesion within P/CROs in Northern Ireland concerning the 'project' as was the case in South Africa. Peace is not generally viewed in such positive/political terms by P/CROs in Northern Ireland, with many groups simply focusing on ending *physical* violence in terms of stopping the killings, beatings and sectarian intimidation. As the later chapters of this book will emphasize, most of the P/CRO groups in Northern Ireland concentrate on the physical *symptoms* of conflict (whether that is represented by paramilitary or state violence), rather than on constructing an underlying philosophy as to its fundamental *causes*.

P/CRO groups in Israel, meanwhile, are cohesive in the sense of regarding themselves as being a part of a broad peace movement. Most of those involved are well-educated, middle-class Israelis, with the bulk of the organizations concentrating on consciousness-raising activities such as public protests and vigils for peace. The Israeli peace groups are also ideologically cohesive, to the extent that (until the signing of the Oslo Accord in 1993) they all rejected the status quo and promoted a policy of accommodation with the Palestinian people. They have always recognized the Palestinian right to self-determination and agreed that the PLO were the legitimate representatives of the Palestinians. Israeli P/CROs have been at the forefront of arguing for a negotiated settlement between Israel and the Palestinians based on 'land for peace'. Their argument, which was eventually accepted by the Israeli government, was that it was in Israel's self-interest to concede land in the interests of security and stability in the region.

Perhaps the greatest paradox within the Israeli P/CRO sector concerns its largely Zionist character,[14] which is both an advantage and a hindrance to its objectives. It has been useful for the peace process because it has helped them to access and influence main-

[14] Curiously, while most of the Israeli peace organizations are critical of the state, they believe that Israel should remain a Jewish state but extend democratic rights of citizenship to the non-Jewish community. T. Hermann, *Israeli Peace/Conflict Resolution NGOs 1967–1998,* Final Report for ISPO, Tami Steinmetz Center for Peace Research, Tel Aviv University, October 1998.

stream Israeli society. However, this has also been a drawback in that it has damaged their access to (and influence within) the Palestinian community, as its largely Zionist image has compounded Palestinian suspicion about the motives of the Israeli P/CRO movement.

> The loyalty of the Zionist peace groups to the Zionist creed clearly left open the way for a more fruitful dialogue with the mainstream and ensured greater success in their mobilisation efforts. However, it was, at the same time, a liability insofar as [it inhibited] their relationships with the Israeli non-Zionist peace organisations, with their Palestinian counterparts for the peace dialogue, and sometimes also with peace movements of radical orientations in other countries. They accused the Zionist peace groups for having no real interest in the peaceful resolution of the conflict and considered their expressions of sympathy with the Palestinian cause devoid of any real content. To counter the Zionist peace groups platform, the Israeli non-Zionist groups, along with the Palestinians, argued that the [sic] these movements and groups serve, even if unintentionally, as a liberal fig leaf, under which the abuses of the Israeli occupation could continue.[15]

This politicization has led to an interesting difference with the situation in Northern Ireland. In Israel there is much less 'cross-community' activity within the peace sector than exists in Northern Ireland, with both Israelis and Arabs tending to 'do their own thing' to a much greater extent.[16] Joint action has been increasing in recent years but it remains at quite a low level. This raises the interesting question as to whether the peace movement in Israel can influence the conflict there, when it cannot even unite the two peace movements?

Another difference between the P/CRO groups in Israel and Northern Ireland relates to their funding. In Northern Ireland, the vast majority of the P/CROs that exist are funded at some level by the British government, including some groups within the republican community that are politically opposed to the British administration but not averse to accepting money from government sources – however indirectly. The Israeli peace sector, in contrast, bears a much closer similarity to the pattern of South African P/CRO funding, as

15 Hermann (1998), pp. 64–5.

16 This trend was exemplified by the fact that within the ISPO project itself, the research was conducted by separate teams of Israeli and Palestinian academics. This does not fill us with hope that the society at a more general level will resolve its differences in the foreseeable future.

most of their resources come from international donors keen to encourage the peace process, rather than from government. This fact has often been used by their opponents in Israel to suggest that the peace movement are the stooges of hostile pressure groups in the international community, politically opposed to the state of Israel. The Israeli government and those close to it have been critical in the past of European Union funding going to P/CROs with an overtly political agenda, such as Peace Now. David Bar-Illan, an aide to the former Israeli Prime Minister Benjamin Netanyahu, declared: 'I find it a bit strange that a foreign government should provide financial support to an openly political organization like Peace Now.'[17]

Not surprisingly perhaps, the picture of NGO and P/CRO development within the Palestinian community differs markedly from that of their Israeli neighbours, despite their geographical proximity. The very term NGO is itself a difficult one. Palestinians have never had a state or a sovereign government of their own; it is difficult to talk about non-governmental organizations when governmental organizations themselves do not exist – notwithstanding the autonomous bodies established within the Palestinian Authority following the Oslo Accord in 1993.[18] Those Palestinian P/CROs that do exist can be separated into two groups. The first were those created before or during the intifada uprising in 1987. These organizations acted as resource centres for their communities and tried to highlight the injustices and hardships imposed on Palestinians by the Israeli Occupation. The second group of organizations were mainly formed after the beginning of the peace process in 1993. The roots of these groups were shallow, and their activity and support has gone up and down in response to political developments. The stuttering nature of the peace process has had a damaging effect on a lot of these organizations; many went into hibernation when Benjamin Netanyahu came to power in 1995 and have not yet fully re-emerged.

The peace and conflict resolution sector is much smaller in Palestine than in any of the other regions examined. The explanation for this is that the Palestinians have felt so oppressed by the Israeli

[17] Hermann (1998), p. 96.

[18] Paper given by Professor Manuel Hassassian, Bethlehem University, leader of the Palestinian research team on the ISPO project, to the Third Conference of the International Society for Third Sector Research (ISTR), Geneva, 8–12 July 1998.

state and so powerless to effect change, they have found it difficult to see the point in opening up a dialogue with those they consider to be their oppressors. As a consequence, the P/CROs within the Palestinian community have concentrated upon delivering services and acting as an alternative government, rather than promoting the values of 'reconciliation' or 'peace'.

From an ideological perspective, the Palestinian P/CROs are similar to their South African counterparts in that few define themselves as pacifist organizations. Most believe in justice *before* peace and are committed to the 'national struggle' in the same way that the South African groups were against the apartheid system.

Clearly then, it is important to understand the political contexts within which P/CROs operate in order to appreciate that their development, underlying philosophies, and the activities undertaken, are products of unique historical environments. The subsequent chapters in this book will illustrate the way in which the P/CRO sector in Northern Ireland was shaped by the specific context of that region's historical and political evolution.

The study of P/CROs in Northern Ireland

Ten organizations within Northern Ireland were selected for analysis following an initial survey of the wider P/CRO community.[19] These ten groups were chosen to incorporate as wide a range of variables as possible along the following indices: size; function; demographic spread; cross-community; inter-community; single-identity; reconciliation; conflict resolution; community development; existing and non-existing. These selection variables are shown in schematic form in Table 1 below.

[19] This survey took place between July and November 1996. The authors examined thirty-six P/CROs by questionnaire, to determine their structure, evolution, ideological focus and range of activities. This survey provided the information to focus the research down to ten organizations for closer scrutiny, while retaining the diversity of the sample.

TABLE 1: SELECTION VARIABLES FOR P/CROs

Orientation	*Structure*	*Focus*	*Size*	*Location*	*Status*
Peace/Rec.	Cross-Community	Explicit	Large	Urban	Existing
Conflict Resolution	Inter-Community	Implicit	Small	Rural	Extinct
Community Develop	Single-Identity				

The main data-gathering instruments for this phase of the research involved a series of semi-structured interviews with members of the participating groups, together with organizational literature that had either been published, or distributed internally.

The ten organizations selected for study in phase two of the project are listed alphabetically in Table 2.

TABLE 2: LIST OF TEN ORGANIZATIONS STUDIED

1	Clogher Valley Rural Development Centre (CVRDC)
2	Committee on the Administration of Justice (CAJ)
3	Dove House Resource Centre (DHRC)
4	Families Against Intimidation and Terror (FAIT)
5	Peace Train (PT)
6	Quaker House (QH)
7	Springfield Inter-Community Development Project (SICDP)
8	Ulster Community Action Network (UCAN Londonderry)
9	Ulster People's College (UPC)
10	Women Together for Peace (WT)

This chapter will conclude with a short section that describes the ten organizations with respect to their formation, mission, geographic location, participant profile and the focus of their activities. It is important to remember that these ten groups are not being evaluated, or compared in the sense of their relative 'worths'. Their function in the chapters that follow is to provide first-hand evidence of the diversity of P/CRO organizations in Northern Ireland, and the manner in which their differing structures, (peace/conflict resolution; cross-community/single-identity, urban/rural etc.) impact upon their philosophies, strategies and activities.

The ten P/CROs: Organization profiles

1. Clogher Valley Rural Development Centre (CVRDC)

Clogher Valley Rural Development Centre is a cross-community initiative that seeks to provide social and economic resources for the Clogher Valley area in County Tyrone. It was established at the end of 1991 by a group of people concerned that the region's peripherality – falling between the major towns of Omagh, Armagh and Dungannon – was having adverse consequences for the development of the Clogher Valley region. When a derelict building became available in 1991, an effort was made to develop it into a community resource. A cross-community aspect was desired because the area was very mixed in terms of its political and cultural complexion, yet there was no one place or facility that could function as a neutral venue to bring both communities together in an unthreatening manner. Funding was applied for from the Central Community Relations Unit (CCRU) and the Community Relations Council (CRC) to help with initial expenses, and a series of public meetings were held to get nominations for the group's first management committee. Today the Centre acts as a community development initiative and a neutral venue for the Clogher Valley area.

2. The Committee on the Administration of Justice (CAJ)

The Committee on the Administration of Justice (CAJ) was formed in 1981 as a civil rights organization with a particular focus on the criminal justice system. The general context related to the deteriorating political situation in the early 1980s and the difficulties presented to the British government of devising and operating legislative procedures for dealing with politically motivated violence within a human rights context. There was a strong feeling among the original activists within the CAJ, that issues of justice and fairness were inextricably linked to the conflict and needed to be addressed if it was to be resolved. There was a desire to draw together a coalition of legal expertise from across the political spectrum to focus on issues surrounding the criminal justice system and the administration of justice, and to make interventions on such issues. It was hoped that the establishment of the CAJ would combat the prevailing tendency to dismiss (or marginalize) people who made interventions around these themes. Today the CAJ has developed this role of legal campaigner against the inadequacies of the criminal justice system, and combined it with a service-delivery function, intervening on individual human rights cases.

3. Dove House Resource Centre (DHRC)

Dove House Community Trust is the legal parent body of Dove House Resource Centre, a building in the Bogside area of Derry which has been used by local community workers since 1984 as an advice facility for the local population. The vast majority of the catchment area of Dove House is represented by working-class Catholics, most of whom would adhere to an Irish nationalist/republican political philosophy. It is a single-identity community development association which focuses on addressing social and economic deprivation in the local area and the needs of its client groups such as the old, the young, women and the unemployed. Dove House contains individuals who, in a private capacity, play a more political role in areas such as contentious parades and policing issues. It currently acts as a community development resource and employs young people on a number of projects.

4. Families Against Intimidation and Terror (FAIT)

Families Against Intimidation and Terror (FAIT) is a single-issue direct-action pressure group. It was formed in 1990 and focuses on highlighting, and trying to stop, paramilitary 'punishment' attacks and intimidation against the civilian population in Northern Ireland.[20] These attacks are normally carried out by both republican

[20] The phrase 'mutilation beatings' was often used by representatives of FAIT during discussions with the authors, to emphasize the criminality of the activity and remove the implicit assumption inherent in the usage of 'punishment beating', that such attacks were in some way a 'just' (if harsh) response to wrong-doing. The attacks themselves vary in nature, often depending on the reasons for them and the nature of those carrying it out. Before the cease-fires in 1994, victims of these 'punishment attacks' would normally be shot through the kneecaps. Failure to appear at the allocated place to receive this summary 'justice' often resulted in victims being shot through the back of the knee rather than the front, resulting in more crippling and long term injuries. After the ceasefires, the number of these attacks increased as paramilitary factions attempted to retain control of their 'turf'. They also changed in nature, with hurley sticks, baseball bats (with or without nails) and even concrete blocks replacing guns as the implements of destruction.

and loyalist paramilitary organizations, in response to what is deemed to be 'anti-social' behaviour such as joy-riding, drug-dealing, or other criminal activities. At times, such beatings and shootings are used by paramilitary groups to enforce their authority and control within urban areas. Those attacked are almost exclusively urban working-class youths. FAIT is both a campaigning organization, lobbying against what it perceives to be human rights abuses and trying to mobilize public opinion over specific instances of intimidation, and a service-delivery organization, acting on behalf of, and providing information for, individuals who approach it for assistance. FAIT claims to be a non-political organization and has members from both sides of the community.

5. *Peace Train (PT)*

The Peace Train formed in 1989 in response to the Provisional IRA's periodic blowing up of the Belfast/Dublin railway line. It constituted itself into two autonomous and legally separate committees in Northern Ireland and the Irish Republic. The first meeting of the Peace Train took place in the Stormont Hotel in Belfast in 1989. The idea was to run trains between Belfast and Dublin to protest at the specific action of the IRA in blowing up the line, and highlight a more general opposition to paramilitary violence. In all, seven Peace Trains ran between 1989 and 1995. The main activists within the Northern Committee were well-known figures from the arts and politics, while the Southern Committee was dominated by trade union activists. At its peak, the Peace Train got several hundred people supporting it in journeys between the two cities. The organization had little impact on the level of IRA bombing that took place either generally or on the railway line specifically. It was gradually overtaken by internal personality clashes and wound up in 1995, though by this time the bombing of the railway line had stopped, following the IRA ceasefire of the previous year.

6. *Quaker House (QH)*

Quaker House is a joint project run by Quaker Peace and Service on behalf of British and Irish Quakers. It is structured in a non-hierarchical way, aided by the fact that it is a small organization with only two staff at any one time, who are normally a married couple of practising Quakers. The group was founded in 1982 in an effort to make a contribution towards reconciliation and justice within Northern Ireland. The work they do is underpinned by the spiritual ethos of Quakerism, which places an emphasis upon finding understanding and respect through dialogue. Quaker House is a terraced building in South Belfast near Queen's University. The main focus of the work that takes place centres on talking and listening to politicians, community representatives and church leaders. On occasion they have also provided the facilities for confidential dialogue to take place between individuals and groups who may not otherwise have met.

7. Springfield Inter-Community Development Project (SICDP)
The Springfield Inter-Community Development Project (SICDP) is a community development organization situated along the interface area bordering North and West Belfast. It is an inter-community group, which works for parallel development within both nationalist and unionist working-class communities. While much of the focus of SICDP work is on socio-economic issues, it sees this regeneration as a first step towards the rebuilding of the communities, and as an essential prerequisite for any subsequent inter-communal rapprochement. The SICDP brings together former loyalist and republican paramilitaries within its management structure, and the current staff leader, Billy Hutchinson, is a leading member of the loyalist Progressive Unionist Party (PUP) and a former Ulster Volunteer Force (UVF) prisoner. The SICDP became formally constituted in 1990 and sees itself as being a catalyst for progressive social change within the communities it deals with, preferring to maintain a low public profile.

8. Ulster Community Action Network – UCAN (Londonderry)
The Ulster Community Action Network, UCAN (Londonderry) was formed during the summer of 1995 in the Waterside area of Londonderry. Its roots lie in the Ulster Community Action Group formed in 1973 as an umbrella organization campaigning for what were perceived to be the interests of the Ulster Protestant community. This organization had itself emerged from the loyalist paramilitary movement. UCAN (Londonderry) therefore, while being an autonomous organization, has its roots in working-class loyalist areas and evolved out of the paramilitary community, though it claims to no longer have any paramilitary connections. Its name was adopted from a shadowy Northern Ireland-wide movement which acted in

the 1970s and 1980s as an umbrella organization, bringing together Protestant working-class business and community leaders on a radical loyalist political agenda. UCAN (Londonderry) is trying to establish itself as a regional version of its older sister organization. It concentrates on providing information and assistance to local community organizations relating to resource acquisition, applying for grant assistance, and working for urban regeneration within the Waterside area. While it claims to be a non-political organization, UCAN (Londonderry) places a great deal of emphasis upon promoting what it sees as its 'Ulster British' heritage and combating what it perceives to be the decline in these values under the inexorable progression of the Irish Gaelic culture. As might be expected from this short description of its evolution, focus and ideology, UCAN (Londonderry) is a 'single-identity' rather than a cross-community organization. It has very limited resources with a small number of committed volunteers and no paid staff.

9. The Ulster People's College (UPC)

The Ulster People's College is a community-based residential educational resource. It has its roots in the community and voluntary sector and emerged to fill a gap which it felt the statutory agencies were not providing for, namely, the low educational attainment and subsequent socio-economic difficulties of urban working-class communities in the Greater Belfast area. It began as a joint initiative from trade-unionists, academics and various community organizations and is now based in one of the wealthiest suburbs of South Belfast. The Ulster People's College claims to 'provide education and training for community development and [to enhance] solidarity between communities'.[21] In addition to its service-delivery function as an educational facility, the Ulster People's College also seeks to contribute to the process of peace and reconciliation through the twin educational programmes of 'community development' and 'democracy and citizenship'. The Ulster People's College began life in 1978, though did not formally constitute itself or run educational programmes until 1982. It has grown from very humble origins with

21 Interview with Representative of Ulster People's College, 10 September, 1997.

no core funding or paid staff, into a moderately sized NGO with an annual budget totalling several hundred thousand pounds.

10. Women Together for Peace (WT)

Women Together for Peace is a reconciliation organization that came into existence in 1970 in response to the rise in sectarian intimidation and violence in Northern Ireland. As its name suggests, it is a gender-specific organization, which attempts to provide a voice for women caught up in the conflict. It started life as a loose collection of autonomous locally-based women's groups, gradually changing into a more centrally led campaigning organization. Women Together began life as a direct-action movement confronting incidents of violence and sectarianism within interface areas of the Greater Belfast region. Their activities were responsive to the environment that surrounded them, so members would go out to clear up after bomb explosions or to stop stone-throwing incidents between rival gangs of youths. The organization also had a significant social element, bringing women out of their houses and providing them with support and solidarity within the context of the group. The main concern of Women Together today is to encourage dialogue, communication and mutual respect between the two main communities in Northern Ireland. It continues to engage in direct action such as holding vigils for peace, and was an active supporter of the political negotations that led to the Good Friday Agreement in April 1998.

These ten organizations were selected for study not because they were better or worse than any others, but because they broadly reflect the structural and ideological diversity of the P/CRO community within Northern Ireland. The following chapters will illustrate how these organizations (and those who participated in them) related to, and impacted upon, the political conflict in Northern Ireland.

2

Origins and Development

One of the central arguments in this book is that the past informs the present within Northern Ireland, not just in the political realm but in the development and orientations of social movements as well. Consequently, it is vital to understand and appreciate the evolution of the P/CRO sector before attempting to assess how such organizations work, or whether they have had a positive impact upon the society within which they operate.

This chapter examines in detail the formation process of ten P/CROs that form the empirical backbone of this research study, in order to determine whether any patterns of evolution exist across the following range of issues.

General context

The historical evolution of 'the third sector' in Northern Ireland is inextricably linked to the development of the state.[1] After partition took place in 1921, the new administration in the North was extremely flat, and operated within a witheringly conservative political culture. From this point until the regime began to disintegrate in the 1960s, there was differential development of an NGO culture within the Protestant and Catholic communities. (See Chapter 3 for a more detailed explanation of this trend.) Due to the political backdrop of constitutional uncertainty during these years, and the centrality of the government at Stormont, (which was always a Protestant and unionist government), there was little space for a

[1] The word 'state' is used here, and throughout the book, for the purposes of linguistic convenience. Its use does not imply that the authors believe Northern Ireland to be a state in the technical sense of the word, as of course it is not.

'third sector' to get off the ground in any coherent or organized sense. The government was, in some senses, a large community development NGO, albeit a politically partial one that sought to develop one section of the population at the expense of another. Despite high levels of poverty and unemployment within the Protestant working class, the prevailing attitude was that the government was the 'provider', the service delivery mechanism for social policy issues. They saw a direct (and for most of the time, benign) cause and effect within the political system between their vote, their concerns, and the activities and social programmes pursued by the government.

The experience of the Catholic community was rather different between 1921 and 1969. There was no allegiance to the state after partition and they felt excluded by the new regime. There is evidence to suggest that many Catholics willingly excluded themselves for ideological reasons, but this has to be balanced by saying that the unionist government did little to encourage Catholics to feel accepted and part of the community. As a consequence of this sectarian evolution of the state, the Catholic community did not look to the 'first sector' at Stormont, but instead developed their own 'third sector' based on community co-operation but infused by a sense of injustice and the political desire to reform the Stormont system of government. As the regime began to disintegrate in the late 1960s amid a rise in sectarian polarization and inter-communal conflict, community action was most recognizable within the political sphere, with the growth of the Northern Ireland Civil Rights Association (NICRA) and its satellite and spin-off groups. Put simply, the engine that drove the evolution of a 'third sector' in Northern Ireland during these years owed less to economics than to the community disagreement over the nature and practices of political institutions.

The social consequences of community conflict, such as changing housing patterns caused by increased segregation, and the displacement of refugees burnt out of their homes, scattered many people to areas with few community facilities or resources. As a result of such dislocation, people fell back on their own means and established groups within their own areas to lobby for action on community development. In some cases these took the form of inclusive self-help groups such as the Credit Union, while other groups formed that took a more confrontational approach, such as the Derry Housing Action

Committee. Paradoxically, such self-help initiatives often precluded any formal community development being undertaken by the state itself, even had it wanted to undertake such a project, which of course its critics said it did not. 'No Go' areas were formed, most famously in 'Free Derry', which came to be dominated not by community workers, but by the paramilitaries on both sides. The breakdown of the state, and the rise in sectarian violence that accompanied this, threw people onto their own resources and forced them in many cases to run their own areas. Vigilante groups such as the Shankill Defence Association were formed in Belfast, while relief centres and transport systems were opened to assist people who had been forced to leave their homes. Community action developed, therefore, in response to political crisis, and not merely out of economic necessity. The evolutionary experience of the NGO sector in Northern Ireland is unique, as it was linked organically to the parallel realities of political instability and politically motivated violence.

From NGO to P/CRO

The first point to make is that the vast majority of P/CROs examined in this study were formed in response to the symptoms of the political conflict in Northern Ireland rather than its causes or perceived causes, whether those symptoms took the form of an escalation in politically motivated violence, a sense of communal deprivation, or a belief that a defined community was losing out, politically, socially, culturally or economically.

The issues of establishment and formation are summarized in Table 3 below. It is evident from this, for example, that most organizations within the sample studied were founded by small groups or even by an individual, in the 1980s and 1990s. Seven of the ten were formed in response to the overall Northern Ireland situation as opposed to some specific event, and the complete set displays a wide range of legal identities and forms. However, it is not the pattern of attributes in relation to the establishment of the organizations that is important, but the range and variety.

UCAN (Londonderry) formally came into existence in 1995 due to resentment among the Protestant community in general, and community leaders in particular, that their concerns over economic deprivation were not being met by funding for local projects and

TABLE 3: ESTABLISHMENT AND FORMATION

	Year	*By whom*	*Why**	*Where*	*How*	*Legal Status*
Ulster Community Action Network UCAN (Londonderry)	1995	Small group	2	NI	Informal	Voluntary community group
Clogher Valley Rural Development Centre	1993	Large group	2	NI	Formal	Development organization
Springfield Inter-Community Development Project	1990	Small group	2	NI Belfast	Informal	Voluntary organization
Peace Train	1989	Small group	1	NI & R.I.	Informal	Pressure group
Dove House Resource Centre	1984	Small group	2	NI Derry	Formal	Registered charity
Committee for the Administration of Justice	1981	Small group	1	NI	Informal	Voluntary association
Families Against Intimidation and Terror	1990	Individual	1	NI	Informal	Company
Quaker House	1982	Small group	2	NI	Formal	Religious organization
Ulster People's College	1982	Small group	2	NI	Formal	Company & regist. charity
Women Together for Peace	1970	Small group	2	NI	Formal	Registered charity

* 1. Specific event (e.g. bombing)
2. Prolonged process (e.g. community tension)

initiatives. There was a belief held by this group of community activists that socio-economic development was not taking place within the grass roots of the Protestant population. Behind this concern lay a general feeling within the Protestant community in the Waterside area of Londonderry that they had lost, or were losing, a way of portraying their culture. It was believed that as they were the minority community within the city, they were consequently losing out at the political, social, economic and cultural levels.

It is interesting that while being a fundamentally different type of organization to UCAN, the general impetus for the formation of Women Together for Peace was similar in nature, in that it emerged out of a concern over the effects of the conflict on the community, and on women in particular. They of course defined 'community' in a different manner to that favoured by UCAN (Londonderry).

Personalities were also critical to group formation. The case of Women Together epitomizes the importance of the 'charismatic leader' in providing the spark of life for the group and becoming the catalyst for organizational development. The Peace People, formed in 1976, is another good example of this trend, epitomized by the personalities of the group's two founders, Mairead Corrigan and Betty Williams. Much of the initial energy within Women Together came from a woman called Ruth Agnew, a cleaner in the Gas Works in Belfast in September 1970. She had a series of dreams about the increasing levels of violence on the streets of the city at the time. Agnew lived in a mixed area and witnessed a lot of her Catholic friends being forced to leave their homes because of sectarian intimidation. The general deterioration of the situation led to the feeling that something should be done by women to try to end the violence. Consequently, the first meeting of Women Together was held in the War Memorial building in Waring Street in Belfast city centre with over 400 women attending from all over the Greater Belfast area. They then set up small groups in the most troubled areas of Belfast such as the Ardoyne, Shankill/Woodvale, Cliftonville, Andersonstown and Suffolk regions. Their activity was not proactive, but responsive to the environment that surrounded them. Consequently, members of Women Together would go out clearing up after bomb explosions, forming human chains in the streets to stop youths throwing stones, and engaging in other forms of direct peaceful protest against violence.

While some organizations formed in response to a general decline in community relations, others had a more focused approach, though this remained within the parameters of the symptoms and products of the conflict rather than addressing its inherent political or historical causes. The Committee on the Administration of Justice (CAJ), for example, was formed in 1981 as a civil rights organization with a particular focus on the criminal justice system. The general context of its birth related to the deteriorating political situation in the early 1980s and the difficulties presented to the British government of devising and operating legislative procedures for dealing with politically motivated violence within a human rights context.

> There was a sense . . . that issues of justice and rights and fairness were part of the conflict and needed to be addressed, and in particular, there were concerns about the impact of emergency law on confidence in the administration of justice. There was a sense that there was a need to build an organization which would draw together people from a wide variety of backgrounds to focus particularly on those issues and to make effective interventions on them, because previously there was a sense that whenever anybody questioned or criticized around these issues, they were marginalized or dismissed, and the Committee set out to establish a group that that wouldn't happen to.[2]

The emergence of the Peace Train organization, which held its first meeting at the Stormont Hotel in Belfast in 1989, again illustrates the way in which a specific by-product of the conflict, in this case the blowing up of the Belfast to Dublin railway line by the Provisional IRA, rather than any analysis as to its inherent causes, was the dynamic behind group formation. When one of the organization's former activists was asked what factors motivated such a diverse collection of individuals to come together at this particular time and on this particular agenda, it was claimed that its genesis was the product of an emotional gut feeling, rather than an intellectual reaction to an intractable political problem. People from a wide variety of political and cultural persuasions came together simply because 'there was something inherently appalling'[3] about the IRA (which espoused Irish unity) repeatedly blowing up the one physical link between Northern Ireland and the Irish Republic.

[2] Representative of the Committee on the Administration of Justice. Interview with authors, 2 June 1997.

[3] Representative of the Peace Train. Interview with authors, 17 June 1997.

> Closer to home, paramilitary organisations in Northern Ireland have exerted considerable influence in their communities by establishing a significant presence within some voluntary organisations. At a more general level some small local groups in Ireland have been thoroughly illiberal in their responses to drug abusers and HIV victims. Pseudo-religious cults, with their internal cultures of intimidation, psychological domination of the individual and sometimes violent agendas, further highlight the dark side of associational life. In a climate of increasing ethnic conflict, manifested in Ireland by communal hostility towards the Travelling community and political refugees, intermediate institutions can be anything but civil.[4]

Several of the organizations studied demonstrate that some groups have more complex formation patterns than others, emerging not simply as a spontaneous emotional reaction to events, but often evolving from previous organizations or community experiences. The origins of the Springfield Inter-Community Development Project (SICDP), for example, illustrate that its foundation was the result of a strategic re-think in a particular area of Belfast, given the experience of community relations work in the region, and a growing view that a community development approach was essential to achieving lasting and sustainable change. The impetus for the foundation of SICDP differs from other groups such as FAIT and the Peace Train, in that it was not a kneejerk response to a specific event such as a 'punishment attack' or a bombing, but was a more fundamental reappraisal of how best to address the social, economic and political issues concerning the community. The SICDP was formally established in July 1990, though it had been informally in existence since 1988. Documentary sources such as the most recent operational plan produced by the Project covering the years 1996–99, together with oral testimony, illustrate that its formation was more a product of trial and error and building on previous experience, than of moral indignation. The initial motivation for formation came when activists from the Ainsworth Community Centre (situated on the sectarian fault line between the Protestant Shankill and Catholic Springfield Roads) became disillusioned at the ineffectiveness of the community relations work that was being carried out in the area. As the following comment illustrates, the founders of the Springfield

[4] F. Powell and D. Guerin, Civil Society and Social Policy (Dublin: A&A Farmar, 1997) p. 24.

Project began to see the 'contact hypothesis'[5] as being fundamentally flawed and undermined by more powerful forces such as community deprivation and alienation.

> This work had entailed cross-community contacts through the provision of children's holidays and 'ghettoway days' when adults and children were taken away for the day to give them a break from the pressures of living in areas of high tension and giving them the opportunity to discuss issues of common concern with people from the 'other side'. Despite friendships being established between some individuals from both sides, it seemed that, despite all the efforts and considerable expenditure over the years, the 'peace wall' was growing longer and higher and tensions between the two communities were worsening daily.
>
> . . . I suppose people were frustrated that no matter what they did, things remained the same. . . . They'd been doing all this work with these kids, taking them away and then they brought them back, and as soon as they brought them back and let them go, it was like letting animals go out of a cage, they went back into the wild and they weren't changed in any way. They were changed for the days that they were away and made friends and all of that, but their understanding soon went away because it was [still] Orangies and Taigs, you know?[6]

However, there was another factor at work here in addition to a strategic re-evaluation. This relates to a point made later in this book concerning the perceived underdeveloped ethos of self-help within the Protestant working-class community. The general feeling amongst the initial activists involved with the SICDP was that there was a need to develop a confidence within the Protestant community, because the Catholic population was organized and had taken a lead in community development. They had developed these skills and structures due to the differential evolutionary pattern of the Catholic and Protestant communities from 1920–72, (explained at greater length in Chapter 3). While the SICDP formed as an inter-community group (working with both Protestants and Catholics simultaneously but separately from one another), its emergence

[5] The 'contact hypothesis' sees community sectarianism as a product of dysfunctional inter-communal relationships and believes that by increasing the amount of contact between the conflict parties (either explicitly in the form of forums for political dialogue, or implicitly via the provision of cross- community holidays, etc.) the negative stereotypical images would be broken down and better relations would emerge.

[6] Representative of the Springfield Inter-Community Development Project. Interview with authors, 13 August 1997.

owed much to this Protestant epiphany, and their realization that they were playing 'catch up' with their Catholic neighbours in terms of community development. Again the issue of personality intrudes here, as the group was a product of a new radicalism within sections of working-class loyalism, particularly from ex-prisoners. As one member of the group recalled: 'The Springfield Project was unique at the time that it came out because it was the first public project that flowed from the Protestant community outward, in terms of a "cross-community" project. It was actually saying to the Catholic community: "We want to raise social issues. We want to look at new concepts."'[7] Like many of the other P/CROs examined, therefore, the spark that gave life to the SICDP, came from the identification of community need, dynamism and initiative from a small group of activists. They had a self-confidence in their ability, and an optimism that their activity could help to make a positive contribution to their defined community.

Different strokes for different folks

The initial focus of the P/CROs examined in this research, reflects the complexity and diversity of the organizations themselves. UCAN (Londonderry) is a good example of a typical single-identity group, with its central focus being simply the operational extension of its birth. UCAN began in the early seventies as a working-class Protestant alliance dedicated to reviving the Ulster Protestant cultural and economic position in urban centres of Northern Ireland. It did not use the UCAN name or adopt a public profile. Instead, the various groups affiliated with it continued to operate under their own autonomous titles. As UCAN initially had no funding, all of these affiliate groups used their own individual resources to engage in any collective programmes. UCAN (Londonderry) emerged out of the umbrella group in 1995 with the specific aim of raising awareness of, and campaigning for, the preservation of an Ulster British/Scots heritage and radical unionist political viewpoint. Their other central goal was to lobby for an improvement in Protestant working-class economic and social conditions in the Waterside area of Londonderry.

7 Ibid.

The focus of *community development* groups, therefore, such as UCAN or SICDP, and single-issue *human rights* groups, such as FAIT and the Peace Train, is very well defined (and at times is self-defining) and differs from other organizations examined in this study, such as Quaker House and the Ulster People's College. These organizations tend to have a looser and more adaptable focus, responding to what they see as changing community needs, rather than lobbying against a pre-identified set of grievances.

Clearly, the main focus of the Peace Train was centred on the IRA bombing of the Belfast/Dublin railway line, though it was stated by some former activists that this specific concern was used as a wider metaphor to expose the flawed logic of paramilitary violence. 'Yes . . . I think most people, myself included, would have seen it as an effective way of focusing attention on the costs which the IRA were imposing. . . . I don't think there were any railway enthusiasts! . . . I think the energy would [have] come from a wider picture of what was happening to Irish society, north and south and . . . dramatizing some of the contradictions in the IRA campaign.'[8] The single-issue focus on the railway link between Belfast (in Northern Ireland) and Dublin (in the Irish Republic) was chosen because of the irony of a republican movement articulating a vision of a thirty-two-county nation, while destroying one of the few geographical and infrastructural links within the thirty-two counties. One former member of the organization's Northern committee recollected that there was a strong consciousness of 'a deep contradiction in the IRA strategy, and this could be highlighted both practically and intellectually'.[9]

Instead of targeting paramilitaries by way of indirect confrontation, as the Peace Train or FAIT tried to do, other P/CROs such as the SICDP took a more conciliatory approach as befitted the different backgrounds of the different organizations. As one member of the Springfield Project declared, the initial focus of the group was grounded in the pragmatism of *realpolitik,* and what was achievable within the context of an urban interface community.

> . . . My argument was that if you wanted to have a community development strategy which went across the two communities, what you really needed to be doing was involving those people who were involved in the

8 Representative of the Peace Train. Interview with authors, 17 June 1997.
9 Ibid.

> conflict, and using ex-prisoners as a type of local hero and . . . saying to [those] people, 'This is the way we should be working'. [People with] street cred. Also, [we had to be] prepared to talk to people in paramilitary organizations, not to ask for their permission to do particular things, but to say to them, 'What do you think of this idea? Do you think this idea is a good one or do you not?' That doesn't mean to say if they say, 'No, it's a totally bad idea, we don't think it's good', that you walked away and didn't do it, but at least you spoke to them, you've found out. Then you try to actually get them to take part in some of the stuff that you're doing, and it worked to a certain degree. . . . The point about it was that paramilitaries needed to be involved, . . . they needed to see that inter-community work wasn't a threat to them. What it was, was I suppose, some form of enhancement of how people lived in that particular community. If they believed that they were the protectors of the people, then they would have to buy into the enhancement of somebody's environment in a sense.[10]

Quaker House on the other hand, is possibly the most extreme example of a P/CRO that evolved with a fluid and adaptable focus, a feature facilitated by the small size of the group and the degree of autonomy it has been given by its governing body. In operational terms, it began as (and remains) a two-person unit, with the freedom to follow where they think the work appears to lead them or where they feel morally compelled to go. Unlike a single-issue human rights group or a community development organization, whose remits are often self-defining, the terms of reference of Quaker House were very open from the beginning. Executive control in the form of a governing body normally came retrospectively, following reports on work that had been done. There was an implicit trust in the staff of Quaker House that they were in the best position to make judgements on the focus and activity of the group, using their 'local knowledge' to make a positive contribution in their work.

> We don't have to, like so many bodies do, simply give a report on what's been achieved against money spent. There is a certain amount of faith that, we're here, and being part of the community, that things will evolve, and we will be led to find the right thing to do. . . . Some organizations are very much under pressure to demonstrate what they are delivering, and I think it is appreciated that by the very nature of what we're trying to do, you can never *measure* the effects in terms of creating relationships between people.[11]

10 Representative of the Springfield Inter-Community Development Project. Interview with authors, 13 August 1997.

11 Representative of Quaker House. Interview with authors, 13 March 1997.

Contrast this ad hoc approach with the original focus of a human rights group such as the Committee on the Administration of Justice (CAJ). The initial focus here was a legal one, reflecting the Committee's initial make-up, as most of those involved came from a legal background. It was not surprising, therefore, that the concerns and expertise of those involved during formation were reflected in the subsequent work of the CAJ. One member of the organization commented that the main focus of the CAJ during its formation amounted to a campaign against the civil liberties and human rights abuses inherent in the existing emergency provisions legislation[12] and the operation of that legislation by the British government: 'I think the initial focus was really emergency laws and the impact of emergency legislation and to apply, [our] legal skills and experience to an analysis of those problems.'[13] Once again, therefore, while the organizational ethos and operational strategy of the CAJ is radically different from other groups within the sample such as FAIT or Women Together, they too were motivated by the symptoms of the political conflict rather than by any overt analysis of its causes, and these (albeit in a legal form) formed the centrepiece of its original activity.

The activists: Touchy-feelies or hard politicos?

The diversity of people involved during the formation process of the P/CROs examined in this research reflects once again the diversity of these organizations within Northern Ireland. However, despite the cross section of social characteristics and political viewpoints, there are a number of common themes that many P/CROs share, which helps to explain why certain types of people joined at particular times. These were a concern about the deteriorating political situation and rise in community, sectarianism; a feeling of responsibility to their community whether that was defined in parochial terms or

[12] The Emergency Powers Act of 1973 related mainly to the introduction of non-jury 'Diplock' courts to try 'terrorist-related' offences, together with new powers of detention for people suspected of committing offences. This legislation became a target of human rights organizations for being draconian and/or counter-productive.

[13] Representative of the Committee on the Administration of Justice. Interview with authors, 6 June 1997.

in the wider sense of Northern Ireland as a whole; an optimism that their activism, when joined with a group of like-minded people, could effect positive change; a degree of self-confidence in their ability to 'make a difference', even if only in a small way, to the social fabric or level of tension/violence within their community.

Obviously, the particular context of the P/CRO is a major determinant in the type of people who join it. The origins of UCAN (Londonderry), for example, lie in the Ulster Defence Association (UDA), the largest Protestant paramilitary organization in Northern Ireland. These antecedents obviously had a direct bearing on the type of people who became involved with the organization. Originally those involved would have been UDA members and others from a similar Protestant working-class background. The sort of people involved in UCAN in its early days in the 1970s were the same working-class loyalists who were involved with the Loyalist Prisoners' Aid group, the Shankill Defence Association, the Loyalist Association of Workers, and other urban working-class Protestant groupings. UCAN, while at that time a loose clandestine grouping, emerged to link these various groups together and provide an overview to their differing perspectives and concerns. Thus UCAN had members who were in the Ulster Volunteer Force (UVF) and who are now in the Progressive Unionist Party (PUP), as well as members of the UDA who have now been politicized into the Ulster Democratic Party (UDP). UCAN also contained people from Ian Paisley's Democratic Unionist Party (DUP) as well as the more mainstream Ulster Unionist Party (UUP). While this may constitute diversity of a sort, clearly the ethos, historical background, geographical location (in the mainly Protestant Waterside area of Derry), and operational focus of the organization, played a large part in determining the type of people who became involved in it. To put it mildly, this was not the sort of organizational profile that a Catholic nationalist would feel an immediate affinity for.

In the same way that the historical evolution of UCAN affected the social profile of its participants, the dynamics that led to the formation of FAIT also moulded its original composition, albeit in a radically different direction. Nancy Gracey and Henry Robinson were the two main people involved at the beginning, together with Sam Cushnahan, a local businessman living in Belfast. Nancy Gracey was the mother of a victim of a punishment attack and became the focus for much of the media attention. Henry Robinson was a former paramilitary prisoner turned P/CRO activist, who like Gracey (though in a different way) provided an initial credibility and media focus for the group. A member of the organization's management committee provided the following explanation for participation in FAIT: 'The sort of people involved in FAIT when it was originally founded were people who had been involved [in], or had suffered from, paramilitary activity. It would definitely have been working class.'[14] Once again the initial motivation for formation, together with the focus and activity of the organization, are the key elements in explaining the social profile of the activists who became involved during the early days of its activity.

The backgrounds of activists within the Peace Train on the other hand differed substantially from those of FAIT, despite the fact that both could be categorized as single-issue human rights organizations. This was partly due to the fact that the issue the Peace Train were focused on (the blowing up of the Belfast/Dublin railway line) impacted on a wider cross section of society than 'punishment attacks', which were normally confined to working-class urban parts of the community. As a result it was easier for the Peace Train to draw in the middle class, and obtain high-profile interest from politicians and consequently the media. While FAIT appealed (in the person of Nancy Gracey) to the integrity/bravery of the 'ordinary citizen' standing up to the violence of the paramilitaries, the Peace Train deliberately set out to attract well-known public faces, particularly within its Northern committee. As in many of the other P/CROs examined during the research, the majority of activists came from a broad left background, as one of the founding members of the organization recollects:

> I think one could generalize [that] it was mainly people from some kind of broad left background. Obviously Paddy Devlin [and] Sam McAughtry [were connected] to the Northern Ireland Labour Party. Seamus Lynch and Mary McMahon [were] also of the then Worker's Party. . . . I'd been a very active member of the Irish Labour Party [Republic of Ireland] and the British Labour Party before coming here [Belfast] and . . . indeed just thinking of Chris and Michael McGimpsey from the Ulster Unionist Party, they would see themselves as [being] on the left of the party.[15]

[14] Representative of FAIT. Interview with authors, 14 March 1997.
[15] Representative of the Peace Train. Interview with authors, 17 June 1997.

It seems clear that the social profile of the original participants is directly related to the historical development of the organization, its initial focus, and how it saw that being achieved. The Springfield Inter-Community Development Project illustrates this fact, as its focus upon socio-economic regeneration and community development within urban interface areas of Belfast denoted the type of people who would become involved in it. One of the founding members of the Project commented that 'They would all have been people who were working class. . . . They would have had twenty years of community development and community work. They all would have understood the concept of community development and would have been involved in initiatives in 1973, which would have been similar to what I was trying to do now.'[16] There would have been little point in the SICDP gathering together a group of people in the manner of the Peace Train, as it was more interested in gaining access to and credibility within targeted working-class areas, than affecting general public opinion through a media-driven publicity campaign. In fact, at one stage during its formation, the SICDP resisted pressure from a funder to appoint well-known political figures to its management committee because this would have sent the wrong message to the people within the communities it was seeking to work with and influence.

Political ideology and P/CROs

The ideological disposition of P/CROs within Northern Ireland is multilayered, reflecting the diversity and complexity of the organizations that exist. While naturally all political attitudes are present, reflecting the wider society from which the activists come, it is possible to say that ideology plays different roles depending on the type of group. Consequently, community development organizations that are cross- or inter-community, such as the Clogher Valley Rural Development Centre or SICDP respectively, will argue that politics 'with a big P' plays no part within the internal organizational ethos or operation of their group. Interestingly, Dove House Resource Centre, a single-identity community group, also claims that political

16 Representative of the Springfield Inter-Community Development Project. Interview with authors, 13 August 1997.

viewpoints on the nationalist/unionist axis are irrelevant, despite the fact that most of those involved come from a similar social and political background. Cross-community reconciliation groups on the other hand, such as Women Together, clearly articulate a more defined ideology somewhere between the unionist and nationalist blocs, that is based firmly on a respect for difference and the need for compromise and forgiveness. In political terms this is closely aligned (theoretically if not in practice) with the Alliance Party, though such comparisons to political parties may not be appreciated by the groups themselves. Perhaps the only common theme in terms of the ideological genesis of P/CROs in Northern Ireland relates not to the orange and green axis but to the red and blue variety. The vast majority of P/CROs and the people who became involved in them during their early evolution came from a broad left perspective. This is the one ideological theme that crosscuts the whole P/CRO sector in Northern Ireland in terms of group type, function and sociological profile. While this illustrates the unpopularity of conservative individualism for the NGO activist, it also highlights the devalued currency of the term 'left-of-centre', which in today's New Labour world of 'third-wayism' accounts for just about everyone!

The ideological position of some single-identity groups, such as Dove House Resource Centre, is complicated by the fact that the division between the socio-economic and the political can at times be an area of some subtlety. While the majority of those involved in Dove House come from the Irish nationalist/republican tradition, this was seen as a matter of private ethics, which did not impinge upon either the organizational ethos or the community development work carried out by the group. A representative from Dove House was asked to outline the balance within the organization between the economic and social regeneration focus and the wider political issues in which it took an interest, such as the Parades controversy. It was pointed out that a simple demarcation between the two did not exist. Social issues such as poverty, poor housing and unemployment were themselves as political as other concerns such as the Parades dispute, the firing of plastic bullets by the RUC and policing policy in general, which were also of central importance to the community Dove House sought to serve.

> If people want to march along the edge of the area and abuse the people, then that impinges upon their social well-being. It also causes a sense of

> outrage, which if not funnelled, would potentially overflow into sporadic rioting and things, which we didn't want, because again, all that does is damage the local community and the local economy and the local people who have invested in business in the area. So, we would have had no difficulty if the manager of Dove House [Donnacha MacNiallais] became directly involved as a spokesperson for the local residents group. The [Bogside] Residents' Group is a separate organization from Dove House.[17]

Single-identity community development organizations such as Dove House will almost inevitably stray into the political arena, driven by an internal ideology that reflects the cohesive communities from which they are derived and which they seek to serve. However, most of these organizations will make a distinction between formal politics 'with a big P' and issue-based interventions reflective of the mood within their client groups. When a spokesperson from Dove House was asked whether the organization had any set of established constitutional ideas, it was pointed out that the group was primarily focused on a geographically specific community, the Bogside and Brandywell area of Derry, and that the focus of its attention reflected the concerns of that community.

> Dove House doesn't have a [political] blueprint. It doesn't set itself up as, you know, either a unionist or a nationalist or a republican or a loyalist organization. But I think because of its location and because of the individuals involved, and because of the history and its interaction with the people in the area, and because of their history of interaction with the state, which has nearly always been in a time of crisis, the individuals involved in Dove House would be representative of the views of the local area, which would be opposed to the state as it is presently constituted.[18]

Other single-identity groups had a much more defined political perspective from the outset. Perhaps the clearest in this regard amongst those studied in this research was UCAN (Londonderry). Their main ideological consideration was to advocate the preservation of the Ulster British heritage. This was the fundamental ideological axis around which everything else revolved. The main focus within that was to provide 'capacity building' within their own defined ethnic community, obtain resources to enable the expression

17 Representative of Dove House Resource Centre. Interview with authors, 17 September 1997.

18 Ibid.

of the Ulster British cultural identity, and secure funding to regenerate the social and economic conditions of those defined as belonging to the Ulster British community. To this extent UCAN was (and remains) a radical organization, with an elaborate critique of the political, social and economic status quo. However, it did not view itself as an overtly party political body. It was claimed that it encompassed 'all political views', though in practice this refers to all *unionist* political views.

Many single-identity organizations exhibit varying degrees of victimhood. This is often why they become established in the first place and forms their central focus, namely to redress the perceived imbalance in economic, social or cultural resources which are available to their defined community. UCAN (Londonderry) provides a classic illustration of this phenomenon, with activists believing that their structural position vis-à-vis the Catholic population is weaker, and that Protestant community development is well behind that of the Catholic population. A UCAN (Londonderry) spokesperson suggested that the nationalist community had a twenty-five-year start on the unionist population in terms of community development, self-help initiatives and obtaining resources for their community. They had the skills, the power base, the contacts and the connections to attract resources, and it was up to the Protestant community to catch up. When asked why this imbalance had come about, the interviewee highlighted the differences between the political culture and religious ethos within the Protestant and Catholic populations. It was suggested that within the Catholic Church there was a collective and single authority which fostered a co-operative spirit throughout that unified body, while the Protestant denominations were multifaceted and splintered. With so many different faiths trying to protect their respective organizations and their own vested interests (e.g. having their followers poached by rival Protestant denominations), it was claimed that much less altruism was available to the Protestant population. The prevailing ethos of Protestantism was also thought to be a barrier to community activism: 'Stand on your own two feet. Expect charity from no one, expect help from no one and do these things yourself.'[19] In comparison to this picture of Protestant religio-cultural

[19] Representative of UCAN (Londonderry). Interview with authors, 25 February 1997.

competition, the UCAN spokesperson believed that within the Catholic community there was a collective church lobby that worked in unison to achieve its goals, which, when translated into the political sphere, meant that Catholics were more cohesive, more effective and thus more successful.

While some may choose to disregard this analysis as being a symptom of paranoid delusion, the important point here is that the *perception* was real, if not necessarily the empirical fact. It is that perception, rather than any objectively measurable reality, that drives single-identity organizations such as UCAN (Londonderry) and similar groups on the nationalist side, and determines their initial goals and activities.

In contrast, as one might expect given the nature of the group, Women Together exhibited a much less evolved ideology than UCAN (Londonderry). As they were primarily concerned with the symptoms rather than the causes of the conflict, and wished to gather together as wide a coalition of women as possible in opposition to violence, an effort was made to minimize ideological differences. The women involved in the organization in the early days came out of their communities; they were normal people from Catholic/nationalist and Protestant/unionist backgrounds and had all of the political and cultural attitudes that one would expect from such people. However, the one thing that united them was their opposition to violence from whatever quarter it came. The common ideological thread within the group was the belief that violence was not a legitimate means to achieve any political objective. Aside from this, the political and cultural background of the participants was reflective of society as a whole. There was no pronounced ideological orientation in terms of socialism, liberalism or even feminism, due to the fact that the group wanted to market itself as a single-issue group dedicated to eradicating violence, rather than an organization with any internal political culture.

Establishing working procedures within P/CROs

The degree of formality within the P/CRO sector concerning the establishment of working procedures varies enormously from the legalistic to the chaotic. Once again the nature of the group and its function played a large part in determining the organizational ethos, with poorly resourced single-issue campaigning groups being often less formalized than core-funded community development organizations. There was often more latitude in the former for the 'gifted amateurs' to coalesce around ideas, while the latter, responsible for delivering community services, had to quickly establish accountable financial procedures. While some of the organizations within our sample, such as the SICDP and the Clogher Valley Rural Development Centre, had quite coherent procedures for joining and leading the group, others such as the Peace Train were much more ad hoc. For example, a representative from the Peace Train was asked how it was decided at the beginning who should take a lead role in the organization. Did they elect a chairperson, a treasurer and a secretary at the outset, or were things more informally arranged?

> It's an interesting question. You'll have to ask Sam [McAughtry] about this. His opening comment was: 'This is the first meeting I've been invited to where I've been told I was elected Chair!' So, my . . . feeling is . . . that it was felt that the Committee here needed someone who would command respect on both sides of the community divide and who would have a fairly high profile, and my guess is whoever did the inviting felt that they had to invite Sam.[20]

It is clear that the initial energies of those actively involved with the Peace Train went into its activities and programmes rather than the structure of the organization. This was not regarded by those who took part as a group that was going to have any permanence and many people gravitated towards it precisely because it had a clearly defined purpose and saw itself as a loose and temporary coalition of concerned people. This had a direct impact on the structural development of the organization in that a hierarchical edifice was not considered appropriate.

Contrast this approach with the formalized mechanisms within Women Together. The evolutionary context is essential to understanding why these P/CROs developed differently. The Peace Train gathered together a wide and disparate coalition of individuals across a range of demographic, political, social and cultural variables. Women Together developed from a much more cohesive foundation, not only in terms of being gender-specific but also with regard to its social base. Women who were strong within the trade union move-

[20] Representative of the Peace Train. Interview with authors, 5 August 1997.

ment also took a leading role within Women Together, and the internal culture of democratic and accountable procedures characteristic of the trade union movement was consequently adopted by the organization. The group was never ad hoc or informal in any way, everything being very structured and transparent. Financial accounts were kept from the first day of formation, while minutes of meetings were maintained and written up assiduously. The AGMs were conducted under scrupulously observed conditions, such as requiring nominations for offices to be submitted weeks beforehand, letters being sent out eight weeks before the AGM, with the nominations being required back four weeks before the meeting, and so on. Many of these women were working in the manufacturing industry in Belfast and wanted to address the conditions of employment they encountered. Many saw the trade union movement as a vehicle to achieve these aims and were thus organizationally literate from an early stage. When they gravitated towards Women Together, they brought this organizational culture with them into the group.

Quaker House lay at the other extreme. Joining and leading within this P/CRO was not an issue as it is not a membership-based organization. It was composed of a Quaker couple[21] who worked in partnership together, and began as an attempt to apply Quaker ideas and philosophies to the conflict in Northern Ireland. The representatives from Quaker House were asked to explain the relationship between the political aspects of the work that was done and the religious element of their activity. Why was it important to be a Quaker in terms of the work that was engaged in? What did Quakers bring to the work that secular groups did not? Was it an attitude of mind, or a matter of how they were perceived by others?

> It's both of those. I think Quakers have always felt that there shouldn't be a sharp distinction between the sacred and secular, that everything you do is religious in a sense. The background is that we don't have any priests, [there is] minimal symbolism, no sacraments, the feeling being that everything you do is part of your religion, and that in fact is important, feeling that it can be a religious calling, just to be here and to be talking to politicians or whatever, as much as other groups would feel the need to go and hold a [religious] Mission somewhere. . . . We think it's important that we are prepared to listen to and respect other people.

[21] At the time the research was conducted in 1997, Alan and Janet Quilley were the Quaker House representatives.

> It's part, I suppose, of our core belief, that there is something of God in everyone if you are prepared to look for it. And that will apply to a member of the paramilitary organizations or politicians whose views you can't stomach or whatever.[22]

It was claimed that there was a democratic ethos within the Quaker movement generally and Quaker House in particular. 'It's very participative . . . we don't vote to make decisions. The theory behind that is that if the meeting is trying to make a decision about something there is a correct decision to be found, God's will if you like, and it's up to us to find it. So there's no point in voting, and if you do, you just exclude the people who lose the vote.'[23] To this degree, Quaker House was unique within the groups in our sample, with an atypical organizational ethos and internal structure.

The target audience of the P/CRO

The different audiences targeted by the P/CRO sector reflect once again the diversity of the groups studied, with some seeking to influence specifically demarcated communities while others sought to target a broader public audience. FAIT clearly tried to look in two directions simultaneously. On one level, it perceived its audience to be the paramilitary organizations that were perpetuating the intimidation and punishment attacks that FAIT had been organized to try to prevent. Consequently, the organization targeted political parties such as Sinn Féin and the Progressive Unionist Party, picketing their offices and leading personnel. On another level, FAIT saw its audience as being the wider community within which the paramilitary organizations operated, and it campaigned through the media in an effort to get its case across to the general public. A leading member of FAIT's management committee was asked to explain who FAIT saw as their primary audience during the formation of the organization:

> The paramilitaries of course and the communities. We wanted to make the communities aware of the type of people that were in their midst. [Also] the media and politicians. We would use the media quite a bit. For instance over the last four years we have been particularly targeting North America, because most people in North America had a very

22 Representative of Quaker House. Interview with authors, 26 March 1997.
23 Ibid.

> romantic version of what was going on in Northern Ireland. They saw 'the Brits' as oppressors, they saw the IRA as the IRISH REPUBLICAN ARMY [his emphasis]. They thought that they were fighting a very just cause . . . and they had a very warped opinion of what actually was going on here, so we decided to put that straight.[24]

For obvious reasons, the target audience of Women Together was more focused than the targets of many of the other groups in the sample during the formation stage. The initial message was very simple: if you were a woman and interested in ending the violence, then you were welcome within the organization. However, while the central aim of the organization was to recruit women members, there were other target audiences relating to the operational goals of the group. The paramilitary organizations were high on the list of targets here, and in the actions they took, Women Together were targeting the perpetrators of violence, while politicians and the media were also lobbied to get the group's case across.

In line with their initial focus, the target audience of Quaker House was non-specific and was responsive to the needs and demands expressed by those they were in contact with. 'People who might have difficulty in meeting other groups of people, who might find the use of neutral space helpful. Usually this would have a political edge to it. It could be [paramilitary groups] yes, or people close to them. People who wanted neutral space which wasn't made public.'[25]

The Ulster People's College, in common with groups such as FAIT, the Peace Train and others, had a number of different audiences that reflected the various aspects of its activity. The College was established as a residential facility and saw itself setting up as a community education college, subsequently marketing itself in this guise. It saw its primary work and core client groups as disadvantaged individuals and communities within society, such as the general working-class population, women's organizations, the disabled, those on low incomes or in poor housing facilities. Its target audience was consequently viewed in broad terms as being the trade union movement and community organizations. In a less direct sense, since part of the College's project was to change mindsets within the community as a whole towards both social policy and attitudes to conflict

[24] Representative of FAIT. Interview with authors, 14 March 1997.
[25] Representative of Quaker House. Interview with authors, 13 March 1997.

resolution, it also saw its audience as being the general population within Northern Ireland. Another key audience for the College was the policy-making community, as the central focus of the organization was to effect change and exert pressure on the power-holders within society. The College has always had a dual focus on delivering a range of services to its client groups around educational issues on the one hand, and campaigning and lobbying against social and political issues on the other, though it had a sharper campaigning focus in its early days than it has now and was more explicitly committed to effecting political change.

As explained above, like many community development organizations, the Clogher Valley Rural Development Centre was not as free as other groups such as FAIT, the Peace Train or Women Together, to select either its initial focus or its audience. A representative of the organization commented that due to its structure and the nature of the work, the group had to mobilize the general community in the Clogher Valley area. Part of the reason for this, aside from using the community as a resource, was that the Development Centre had a defined catchment area and was therefore necessarily responsive to the needs (and wants) of local people. To that extent, it evolved as a bottom-up organization and developed its programmes in reaction to what the community felt was needed in the locality.

> We were starting from a blank page. So, we didn't turn up and say, 'Right, we'd better do something to do with farming', although the reason why it keeps coming up is because it is the key employer in the area. It was more a matter of trying to sit down and see what could be done from scratch with a blank page. . . . There's a large agricultural programme about to start, which would involve not just farmers, but farm families, farm wives, farm children. . . . So it's not just farmers, you know. If we're involved in a project I'm afraid we have to try to go 'the whole hog' and bring as many people in as possible, so [we initially targeted] the general population.[26]

Like the Clogher Valley Rural Development Centre and Dove House Resource Centre, the Springfield Inter-Community Development Project was very much rooted in a geographically defined catchment area, which made the group's target audience self-selecting.

[26] Representative of the Clogher Valley Rural Development Centre. Interview with authors, 28 May 1997.

> It was from Divis Street up to the corner of the Whiterock [Road]. It was very much [aimed at] people who were alienated, marginalized, whatever [term] you want to use. Very much people who were 'under the cosh' in terms of being politically excluded and socially excluded, and those were the people that I went for, because I felt at that time that they were the people who needed an inroad, and that this was the opportunity to give them, whereas if I had gone for others who were already accepted by civil servants and accepted by government, then they might not have had as much interest in working with me.[27]

The interviewee commented that those who became active within the organization and who participated in its activities and programmes would have been those suffering from social exclusion and disadvantage. 'They would have been long-term unemployed people, they would have been ex-prisoners, they would have been women who were involved in women's groups where their kids were being . . . tortured by all sorts of adults, whether it was teachers, policemen, or paramilitaries, and the kids just were totally marginalized because of it, you know – they were being punished by everybody.'[28]

As can be seen from the following response of a founding member of the Peace Train organization (a campaigning single-issue group rather than community development body), they had a much more complex set of target audiences when they formed than was evident within the initial focus of groups such as the Clogher Valley Rural Development Centre, Dove House or the SICDP.

> I think the media weren't a target audience, but certainly we saw the media as enormously important in terms of radiating our message [and] amplifying it, and I think the whole campaign was quite media-oriented, not least I think because the Peace Train idea was a fairly imaginative one and had visual [impact] . . . and an element of dynamism as well, so it was a good set of images to, in a sense, exploit. I think initially the target audience was the general public. One of our concerns was that, inevitably I think, there is a tendency to sink into apathy. The rail line being blown up regularly just becomes like part of the weather as it were, you kind of accept it as a way of life and you accept other things and, you know, you go on accepting what is normally unacceptable as part of living in the society. So I think it was to jolt people out of that apathy. I would have seen that as perhaps one of the primary objectives and the general public as the key audience. I don't think we had any notion of

27 Representative of the Springfield Inter-Community Development Project. Interview with authors, 13 August 1997.

28 Ibid.

> influencing the IRA or Sinn Féin for that matter, directly, in a sense that they were going to sit around a table and think, 'Well lads, these people have rightly exposed certain contradictions in our position, let us reconsider'. But we did feel that we might be able to embarrass them. In a sense it's [a] confrontational approach.[29]

The notion of target audiences is closely allied to ideas about what the fundamental or long term intentions of the organizations are in respect of influence and impact. Table 4 indicates how the ten organizations examined in detail during the course of this research, responded to a set of possible goals, including education and influence on government policy.

The least popular of these goals, with only four of the ten groups supporting it, was 'changing the political system'. This reflects other views expressed during this research about the lack of a fundamental political analysis of the conflict (see Chapter 4), and also a perception that social (or community) rather than political activity is the central task which the organizations feel they have to accomplish. All ten groups indicated the existence of another goal in addition to those named in the table, which supports the view that all such organizations are to a degree unique and singular in many aspects of their fundamental make-up.

Show me the money . . .

The last issue of commonalty to discuss in this chapter brings us back full circle, in that attitudes to funding run in parallel to the whole organizational ethos of the P/CRO sector. Clearly, a group cannot evolve without acquiring resources to fund its activities and this is quite often the single largest preoccupation within the organization after the P/CR focus that caused it to form in the first place. (See Chapter 6 for a more detailed account of funding issues as they pertain to P/CROs today.) There appears to be a remarkable degree of uniformity across all variables, between community development and reconciliation groups, cross-community and single-identity organizations, middle-class and working-class groups, and rural and urban groups. In terms of understanding the evolution of the P/CRO sector (rather than how it operates today), it is clear that questions of

[29] Representative of the Peace Train. Interview with authors, 17 June 1997.

TABLE 4: GOALS

	Education	*Influencing public opinion*	*Changing government policy*	*Changing political system*	*Changing social structure*	*Other*
Ulster Community Action Network UCAN (Londonderry)	Yes	Yes	Yes	Yes	Yes	Yes
Clogher Valley Rural Development Centre	Yes			Yes	Yes	Yes
Springfield Inter-Community Development Project		Yes	Yes		Yes	Yes
Peace Train		Yes				Yes
Dove House Resource Centre	Yes		Yes		Yes	Yes
Committee on the Administration of Justice	Yes	Yes	Yes	Yes	Yes	Yes
Families Against Intimidation and Terror		Yes				Yes
Quaker House	Yes		Yes		Yes	Yes
Ulster People's College	Yes	Yes	Yes	Yes	Yes	Yes
Women Together for Peace	Yes	Yes	Yes		Yes	Yes

funding were nearly always a secondary consideration to the people who established the groups. The prevailing attitude at formation was often best expressed as a 'can do' spirit and a belief that the money would be found somewhere. This perhaps reinforces the evolutionary patterns discussed earlier in this chapter, in that individuals became motivated by the symptoms of political conflict in Northern Ireland rather than the causes, and specifically, its human costs. The motivation therefore was often *emotional* rather than *political* and a feeling that something, however small, had to be done to change things, whether that was based on a community development, reconciliation, or human rights agenda. This 'gut reaction' which provided the initial spark for most of the P/CROs studied, was based on an incrementalist vision for many of the pioneering activists. They would do *something* even if they had no resources; if they received some funding they would do a little more, and so on. Consequently, few of those involved at the outset thought it necessary to put a funding structure in place before establishing their organizations. From a more general perspective, the cooperative spirit and self-help ethos inimical to the NGO sector, fed into this organizational culture and encouraged the participants to act first on the merit of the idea and think about funding issues subsequently. The general personality profiles described above, of self-starting, driven, optimistic individuals given to idealism rather than cynicism, also contributed to this evolutionary pattern within the P/CRO sector.

The sample of organizations examined in the course of this research study clearly demonstrated this pattern of development, notwithstanding variations resulting from individual structural contexts. Quaker House, for example, was rather anomalous in this regard as it was core-funded from the outset by a central Quaker body, making funding secure and issues of financial resources extremely minor. Funding was not a particular worry for UCAN (Londonderry) either, as it had survived without any money and existed on the voluntary effort of committed people. UCAN was helped in this by its structure as an umbrella grouping, because resources would be provided as necessary by individual groups affiliated to it. The organization's evolution has therefore been based largely on self-finance within the Protestant population. UCAN is proud of the fact that the organization is not dependent upon any individual for survival. A spokesperson declared that this was a symptom of the 'work ethic' within the Protestant population: 'We are self-sufficient, totally independent and belong to nobody.'[30] The UCAN position is that it is not prepared to compromise the work that it does, or shift the focus of that work in response to funding influences or the agendas of funding agencies: 'We will do what we do, and be damned for it, rather than acquiesce [in] someone else's agenda.'[31]

A similar evolutionary pattern is evident within Women Together, who did not give much thought to funding issues at the outset. They started in response to a demand within the community and did what they could within the resources that were available to them. There was no formal funding at the beginning and nobody appeared to be unduly worried about it, partly because there were more important issues at hand such as the imminent breakdown of social order. Women Together did not employ a part-time secretary until it got some funding from the government's Central Community Relations Unit in 1985–86. Unlike a community development organization with an ongoing service delivery function, the overheads of Women Together were extremely low at the outset. For a long time there were no permanent premises, with meetings being held in members' houses. Later, when they had a small amount of funding, Women Together got a room in Bryson House (a converted toilet) in Belfast, for which they had to pay a rent for the privilege of using.

The story of the CAJ is similar, in that the organization evolved from small, humble and inexpensive beginnings. It is clear that funding was not a major problem at the outset because the organizational infrastructure and overheads were minimal. 'There was no money and, I mean, to a large extent in that early period the Committee relied on the Peace People for administrative support and they would have had their meetings in the Peace House between 1981 and 1985, and conferences would have largely been self-financing with money put together from fees from people attending.'[32]

30 Representative of UCAN (Londonderry). Interview with authors, 25 February 1997.

31 Ibid.

32 Representative of the Committee on the Administration of Justice. Interview with authors, 26 May 1997.

The pattern of the Peace Train's financial evolution was identical, with the motivation to carry out activities dominating practical questions about feasibility and funding. A representative of the Peace Train was asked whether the group simply emerged from an emotional 'gut reaction' because people believed that something had to be done, and they then looked around for money to do it afterwards? 'Yes, absolutely. It was in that order. Finances took a very low priority. I mean obviously we sought funding, but I think it was the idea and the motivation [that came first]. People were determined this was going to happen and [thought] the campaign would generate its own finances somehow.'[33]

The above evidence would suggest that P/CROs developed primarily due to a sense of urgency and a radical energy/emotional zeal in a group of committed individuals. Few of those involved at the beginning seemed to be concerned with matters of accountancy, or to consider whether the organization would be sustainable over time.

The end of the beginning

This chapter has demonstrated that the ways in which P/CROs evolved during the period from 1969 were inextricably linked to the specific contexts which surrounded their births, combined with their structural positions vis-à-vis community development/reconciliation/conflict resolution. The overriding theme that emerges is that most came into being because of the consequences of political violence in Northern Ireland rather than due to any analysis of its underlying causes. This is a theme that will be reinforced in Chapter 4, when specific attitudes to the conflict are examined in detail. The concern with the human costs of violence shaped the strategies which the groups adopted, the activities they sought to engage in, the type of people who joined, and the original funding cultures which prevailed in many of the P/CROs. In other words, this concern with symptoms rather than causes produced a discernible evolutionary pattern within the P/CROs studied and left an indelible imprint upon their subsequent development and activities. Kate Fearon of the Northern Ireland Women's Coalition, reflects on the

[33] Representative of the Peace Train. Interview with authors, 15 August 1997.

genesis of these P/CRO movements in the 1970s. Her conclusions are astute and injected with a stiff dose of realism:

> In the beginning . . . all politics was local and informed largely by the self-help ethic established in response to appalling social conditions and then to the conflict. Lunch groups for the elderly, playgroups for children, holiday exchange programmes. Nothing too radical. Nothing too political. Many commentators have viewed much of this as naive romanticism. It had no real impact on conflict resolution. Insofar as this goes, it is true. But to be fair, the people who were organising these activities should not be responsible for resolving constitutional conflict – and not all of them claimed to do so. In the seventies, perhaps stabilising communities was radical enough.[34]

The remaining chapters of this book will concentrate on the debate surrounding the P/CRO sector: What did these individuals and groups do during the last thirty years of community conflict? How did they do it? Most crucially, did their work actually make any difference to the political 'peace process' in the 1990s that culminated in the 'settlement'[35] represented by the Good Friday Agreement of 10 April 1998?

34 Kate Fearon, *Fortnight*, September 2000, p. 26.

35 The word 'settlement' is used with regard to the Good Friday Agreement in the knowledge that there are some people in Northern Ireland (and outside), of both unionist and republican views, who do not regard it as such, and are politically opposed to it.

3

Background to the Conflict and the Relevance of Voluntary Action

This chapter will give a brief overview of the political, social, economic and cultural factors that played a part in the emergence of the Peace/ Conflict Resolution (P/CRO) sector within Northern Ireland. This will provide a contextual narrative for the specific ideologies, activities and focuses of the P/CROs that will be examined in subsequent chapters.

The following quotation, taken from one P/CRO studied, illustrates that a recognition of the historical inheritance and political context of the region is crucial to an understanding of why such organizations evolved:

> I think one of the earliest things was getting people to be aware of their position and what sort of rights they basically had. That would include everything from rights in terms of people's situation [vis-à-vis] the conflict. [For example] if they had a son or a daughter arrested, or if the house was raided, [we would inform them of] what their rights were. Also then [in terms of] welfare rights, if someone had a sick or invalid relative [we would inform them] of what rights were available to them.[1]

Historical background

It was once remarked by Oscar Wilde, that Irish history was something Irishmen should never remember and Englishmen should never forget. Perhaps it is unfortunate that the converse is usually the case. History lives in Ireland, or more especially in Northern Ireland,

[1] Representative of Dove House Resource Centre. Interview with authors, 9 October 1997.

because the issues and disputes that form the dynamics of the present conflict are seen as merely the latest round in an ancient and historic struggle. The questions about ethnicity, territoriality, power and national identity, which have determined the region's historical development, have not yet been resolved, though the Good Friday Agreement of April 1998 is undoubtedly the most concerted effort to do so. As a result, the past is invested with an importance that is not reflected in more stable societies, where the commemoration of battles is restricted to the cultural realm. History is often used within divided societies (and Northern Ireland is no different in this respect from other contested regions such as the Middle East), not as a means of understanding the past, but as a weapon in a contemporary argument. As a consequence, history, and the recollection of that history, has become skewed by two competing communities, each anxious to prove that the past legitimately underpins their present political allegiance and behaviour. It would be fair to say that in Northern Ireland the past is not really 'past' at all, but informs (and at times infects) the political and cultural perspectives of the communities that live in the region. This chapter will illustrate that the P/CRO sector in Northern Ireland, like the political parties and patterns of tribal voting behaviour, is a product of a political conflict driven by contested versions of that past.

Northern Ireland was formed after the signing of the Government of Ireland Act in 1920. This in effect partitioned Ireland into two different administrations, and it remains at the heart of the political conflict today. Twenty-six of Ireland's thirty-two counties were effectively given autonomy from Britain and became known as the Irish Free State (it was not until 1949 that the region became formally constituted as the Republic of Ireland). The remaining six counties in the north, with a majority Protestant and unionist population, were permitted to remain within the United Kingdom and granted a regional parliament to administer the domestic affairs of the area.

An imposing parliament building was constructed at Stormont on the edge of Belfast in the 1930s and this became the seat of government for the Unionist Party until the parliament was prorogued in 1972.[2]

[2] Stormont once again became the home of devolved government in Northern Ireland following the Good Friday Agreement of April 1998 and the establishment of its various institutions.

The relationship between the Protestant/unionist and Catholic/nationalist communities became the main axis of conflict within the Northern Ireland state. Nationalists felt that they had suddenly been politically and culturally marooned by partition, cut off from their Irish counterparts on the rest of the island and left at the mercy of their unionist enemies. As a consequence, many rejected the new political regime, refused to participate in public life, and turned inwards for economic and social support. This development of a quasi-state by the Catholic community began a self-help culture that was not matched within the Protestant community, and led eventually to the development of community-based initiatives such as the credit union and other NGOs in the 1960s. As the same sense of political and economic grievance did not exist within the Protestant community, which looked to the Stormont and Westminster governments for leadership, community and voluntary organizations were much slower to develop.

While the Protestant/unionist community did not want Ireland partitioned either, they soon recognized the potential benefits of the new regime. They were faced with the unenviable task of constructing a political regime in the face of latent antagonism from the British government and periodic aggression from nationalists in the Free State and within Northern Ireland itself. From the earliest years of the administration therefore, the political culture within the unionist community was dominated by fear and uncertainty, and this was reflected in political, social and economic policies within Northern Ireland. Despite the inclusive rhetoric of Sir James Craig in June 1921 – 'We will be cautious in our legislation. We will be absolutely honest and fair in administering the law'[3] – the unionist leadership soon found it imperative to engage in a populist form of government that appealed to its core support while alienating the nationalist community. Their experience was that, far from constructing an inclusive democratic polity, the unionist government was antagonistically anti-Catholic, anti-nationalist and, due to the electoral arithmetic that gave unionists a comfortable majority in parliament, was likely to remain in power for a considerable period of

[3] Sir James Craig speaking on 23 June 1921, shortly after he became Northern Ireland's first Prime Minister. Patrick Buckland, *James Craig* (Dublin: Gill and Macmillan, 1980), p. 51.

time. As a consequence of the resulting disillusionment, the nationalist community began to develop coping mechanisms in the form of self-help initiatives and community-based organizations. These eventually provided the infrastructure and leadership for the civil rights movement in the 1960s.

The unionist perception meanwhile was that they were under siege from a range of hostile forces, from a duplicitous British government to an irredentist neighbour in the South, which openly claimed in its 1937 constitution that the six counties of Northern Ireland were part of its 'national territory'. Such a perception produced a desire for political domination. It was believed by many Protestants that if the Unionist Party lost control of government, then the whole Stormont regime would collapse and they would eventually be subsumed, politically, culturally and religiously, into a united Ireland dominated by conservative Catholicism.

Conversely, the political perception within the nationalist community after 1920 was that they were being trapped within a state to which they held no allegiance, and were being treated there as second-class citizens under the law. Almost overnight, they had been transformed from a majority in pre-partition Ireland, into a minority within Northern Ireland. This nationalist sense of grievance over how the state was managed was essentially a pragmatic judgement born out of experience, rather than a dogmatic or fundamental ideological objection to how it was constructed. The inadequate reaction of successive unionist governments to nationalist alienation, and eventually their inability to reform the political regime, led to an increase in community activism, the growth of the civil rights movement in the 1960s, and subsequently to state breakdown and the outbreak of political violence in 1969.

The political architecture of Northern Ireland was designed to ensure that a stable unionist majority existed that would be capable of discharging local government responsibilities. However, the existence of a sizeable Catholic minority, too large to be assimilated but too small to exert substantial political influence, ensured that ethnic friction would play a central role in the political development of the region. As James Loughlin has succinctly observed of partition, 'However sensible this arrangement for resolving the Ulster question may have seemed at the time, it was inherently flawed, while the treaty in general would initiate a conflict that allowed the consequences of those flaws to be magnified'.[4] As nationalist and unionist polarization increased, elections became more a surrogate census than a democratic competition between alternative ideologies. As one commentator has pithily commented: 'Elections are less about casting your vote than voting your caste.'[5] While Northern Ireland has often seemed in recent years to be the acme of political instability (at least until the establishment of the devolved structures under the terms of the Good Friday Agreement), between 1920 and 1972 it was stable to the point of sterility. In a fifty-two-member parliament, the Unionist Party never held fewer than thirty-two seats, while individual seats themselves often went uncontested. For example, between 1929 and 1969, 37 per cent of all seats were unopposed.[6]

The breakdown of the Stormont regime, which had witnessed one-party unionist government from 1920 to 1972, was linked to a rise in sectarian violence and the increasing conflict between the mainly Catholic civil rights movement and a unionist community frightened by the implications of political change.

The main grievances of the Catholic community centred on abnormally high levels of unemployment, the lack of an equitable system of housing allocation and electoral malpractice. In Derry City, for example, unemployment stood at 20 per cent in 1967, compared to a United Kingdom average of 2.5 per cent and a Northern Ireland average of 8 per cent. The Northern Ireland Civil Rights Association (NICRA) was formed in 1967 and a series of non-violent parades and protests attempted to effect change by embarrassing a unionist government formally committed to a reform policy. This unwillingness on the part of the Catholic community to remain passive until reforms were delivered produced a corresponding reaction within radical sections of the unionist population. Many unionists saw the civil rights movement not as an attempt to redress economic, social and political grievances, but as an effort to destabilize and overthrow the state. New unionist leaders such as Ian Paisley emerged during this period and capitalized on the increased sense of fear and insecu-

[4] James Loughlin, *The Ulster Question since 1945* (Studies in Contemporary History, Basingstoke: Macmillan, 1998), p. 14.

[5] John Darby, *Scorpions in a Bottle* (London: Minority Rights Group, 1997), p. 58.

[6] P. Arthur and K. Jeffery, *Northern Ireland since 1968* (London: Blackwell, 1988), p. 33.

rity within that community. The first of the contemporary paramilitary organizations (that is, those that became protagonists in the current phase of political conflict from 1969–2000), the Ulster Volunteer Force, was formed in 1966 as a reaction to what many radical unionists considered to be an attack by nationalists on the political system.

Increasingly, the Northern Ireland government became squeezed between the demands of the civil rights movement and the impatience of the British government for political reform. Having partitioned Ireland, the preferred policy of successive British governments was to ignore the region. In hindsight, this can been seen to have been a sanguine, short-term and foolhardy political strategy. While London was successful in diminishing Northern Ireland's importance within its domestic political agenda after 1972, and had neutralized it to a great extent as an issue of international (and particularly American) concern, it had not resolved the inherent causes of tension within the region. As successive British governments could not understand the reasons underlying community sectarianism in Northern Ireland they chose to ignore them, with disastrous results. James Loughlin points out the importance of the government's 'out of sight, out of mind' approach to the eventual breakdown of the Stormont system in the late 1960s, and suggests that they had been living in something of a 'fool's paradise' since partition in 1920.

> Ireland as a complicating factor in British politics had been removed while at the same time it was kept within the empire. In the process the international aspect of the Irish question – especially in its Irish-American aspect – had been neutralised. Nevertheless, this was to solve the Irish question – or the Ulster question as it would in future be chiefly known – only in its 'external' aspects, and it was only achieved at the cost, over time, of intensifying its 'internal' dimensions. Probably the most important factor that facilitated this process was the resolute refusal of British politicians to become involved in Northern Ireland's affairs.[7]

The rise of sectarian violence and, in particular, coverage by the broadcast media of a British police force (the Royal Ulster Constabulary) seeming to act in a partisan manner, by attacking

[7] Loughlin (1998), p. 18.

unarmed and peaceful civil rights protesters, was a severe embarrassment to the British government.

In August 1969, unable to contain the deteriorating situation, the Northern Ireland administration asked the Westminster government to send in the British Army to contain the rapid escalation of sectarian violence. While the army was initially accepted as a peacekeeping force by the nationalist community, the relationship between the two sides soon changed. Despite taking the decision to deploy British troops in the region, Westminster remained reluctant to assume political responsibility. The result was that the British Army came under the executive control of the Northern Ireland government – in other words, the Unionist Party. This, in effect, politicized the British Army in the conflict and established clear lines of confrontation with the Irish Republican Army (IRA).

The political landscape was complicated in the early 1970s by the formation of new political parties, such as the moderate nationalist Social Democratic and Labour Party (SDLP) in 1970. That year also saw the formation of the Alliance Party of Northern Ireland (APNI), while in 1971, the radical Democratic Unionist Party (DUP) led by Ian Paisley was formed. The political situation continued to deteriorate and initiatives designed to contain the violence, such as the introduction of curfews in Belfast in 1970, and internment without trial in August 1971, only succeeded in further inflaming sectarian tensions. While the army was initially perceived by the Catholic community as having a peacekeeping role, and was welcomed as a force of law and order that would protect them from being intimidated and forced out of their homes by loyalist mobs, its enforcement of the Stormont government's policies quickly tarnished its image within the Catholic population. As the army was in the front line, imposing policies such as curfews and internment in the early 1970s, it was perceived not as an impartial protector but as a brutal enforcer of policies devised by the unionist government. The following recollection of the period from a Catholic resident of Belfast's Ardoyne, in Fionnuala O'Connor's book on Catholic opinions in Northern Ireland, is typical of how opinions changed towards the army due to negative experiences of its behaviour:

> I was in Toby's Hall and a British foot patrol came in – one soldier opened fire and shot a fella dead. This would have been late 1970. I wasn't allowed to go there but I went to meet a fella. I was sitting with a

> few friends and this patrol came in. A normal occurrence; they'd have harassed a few people, shoved a few around, anything to upset your night's entertainment. This night they appeared to be kind of drunk and they demanded drink. And of course, being a republican area, obviously they weren't given any. A few people started banging bottles of beer on the tables and shouting, 'Out! Out! Out!' and then one person threw an empty glass and it smashed on the floor beside them. Well, one soldier lost his nerve . . . he turned full circle and opened fire while he was turning. There were soldiers outside as well and when they heard the shooting inside, they started shooting from outside in. It was only a prefabricated hut. I can't believe there wasn't a massacre. People just shoved everybody down on to the ground and lay there – and it seemed as if there was a million bullets flying around. I remember thinking, when I look up everybody's going to be dead. . . . The soldiers left and everybody was shouting and crying – pandemonium. And there was a fella lying dead. . . . When I opened the door, there were the soldiers, all lined up, down on their hunkers with their rifles pointed towards the door. And I thought, they're going to shoot us one by one. They had to practically pull me out of the place.[8]

By 1970 the battle lines had been established and the scale of sectarian clashes between loyalists, republicans and the British army began to escalate dramatically. The following table indicates the pace of the political disintegration that was taking place.

TABLE 5: DETAILS OF VIOLENCE 1969–72[9]

Year	*Deaths*	*Bombings*	*Shootings*
1969	13	8	0
1970	25	170	213
1971	174	1,515	1,756
1972	467	1,853	10,628

Community responses

One of the first observable forms of community organization during this period was the formation of the main paramilitary groupings within nationalist and unionist urban areas, particularly in Belfast and Derry. While the IRA had not formally gone out of existence

8 F. O'Connor, *In Search of a State: Catholics in Northern Ireland* (Belfast: Blackstaff Press, 1993), pp. 10–11.

9 These figures are taken from P. Bew and G. Gillespie, *Northern Ireland: A Chronology of the Troubles 1968–1993* (Dublin: Gill & Macmillan, 1993).

prior to the outbreak of political conflict in the late 1960s, it had become moribund and inactive. The IRA split at the beginning of 1970 with the emergence of the Provisional IRA, who advocated a more intensive military campaign against the British and sought to act as 'defenders' of Catholics who were being burnt out of their homes and intimidated by loyalists in Belfast. On the unionist side, the Ulster Volunteer Force (UVF) had formed in 1966, while the Ulster Defence Association (UDA), a larger grouping of urban working-class males, emerged in September 1971. This acted as an umbrella organization bringing together a range of Protestant vigilante groupings such as the Loyalist Association of Workers (LAW) and Shankill Defence Association, in response to a desire for more coordinated action against the Provisional IRA and to prevent attacks on Protestant civilians. Many of the activists within the P/CRO sector in Northern Ireland are veterans of this period, and some became involved in paramilitary activity at this time. One of the organizations studied during the course of this research, the single-identity loyalist UCAN (Londonderry), has its roots within the UDA, while the cross-community organization Women Together for Peace was formed in reaction to the rise in sectarian violence that characterized the period.

It may seem anomalous that many of those who are today engaged in reconciliation and/or conflict resolution activity, were themselves once actors in that conflict. This apparent paradox can be explained, however, by the fact that the type of people who were attracted to re-building their communities during the late 1990s, and who are anxious to build a more constructive polity under the terms of the Good Friday Agreement in the early years of this century, were also anxious to 'defend' those same communities from perceived attack in the early 1970s. In that sense, the formation of both sets of paramilitary groups was an act of community organization, identical in motivation, though obviously differing substantially in ideology and activities, to the community development initiatives that exist within Northern Ireland today.

It was clear by the end of 1971 that the Northern Ireland government was not capable of containing the conflict militarily or introducing the necessary political reforms that might reduce its causes. The *coup de grâce* for the Stormont administration came on the 30 January 1972, 'Bloody Sunday', when British paratroopers killed fourteen unarmed civilians during a civil rights march in Derry. This sent a wave of revulsion around Ireland and brought ignominy upon the British government from international public opinion. The strength of feeling generated by 'Bloody Sunday' was epitomized by Bernadette Devlin, Westminster MP for Mid-Ulster, in a speech during a House of Commons debate when she attacked the Home Secretary, Reginald Maudling:

> The Minister has stood up and lied to the House. Nobody shot at the paratroops, but somebody will shortly . . . I have a right, as the only representative in this House who was an eyewitness, to ask a question of that murdering hypocrite' [Maudling]. She then ran across the floor of the House, pulled Maudling's hair and slapped his face. Later she said, 'I did not shoot him in the back, which is what they did to our people'.[10]

The international condemnation that accompanied Bloody Sunday forced the British government to take political responsibility for Northern Ireland. In March, Stormont was prorogued and direct rule from Westminster introduced, with a Secretary of State and a team of junior ministers carrying out responsibilities previously exercised by unionists at Stormont. For the next twenty-eight years, British government policy would combine attempts to contain sectarian violence with efforts to devise political structures capable of finding some degree of cross-community support between the unionist and nationalist populations.

As with partition before it, the introduction of direct rule was a pragmatic rather than an ideological policy, regarded by the British government as being the 'least worst' option, and a short-term initiative designed to deal with a particular emergency, namely the breakdown of political legitimacy and consequent rise in politically motivated violence. The effective permanence of direct rule has had a major impact on the development of politics in Northern Ireland amongst the élites and on the development of local community activism within the Catholic and Protestant communities. Aside from the obvious point that a degree of power and patronage was removed from the unionist community (or, more accurately, the Unionist Party), the introduction of what was, in effect, government by remote

[10] Hansard, Vol. 830, cc. 37–43. Quoted in Bew, P. and G. Gillespie (1993), p. 45.

control, left a 'democratic deficit' in the region. No longer responsible for public policy or delivering services other than those represented by the 'three-Bs' at local government level, namely 'bins, bogs and burials', the main political parties contented themselves with indulging in a destructive critique of government policy and one another. The seemingly endless procession of elections throughout the 1970s and 1980s, together with attempts to massage the political stalemate via inter-party talks, saw an emphasis being placed upon the constitutional future of Northern Ireland, while pressing social and economic issues slipped down the policy agendas of most parties. Crucially, politics within Northern Ireland became disconnected from the process of day-to-day government. Although the polity may have been largely corrupt between 1920 and 1972, there was at least a rational chain of cause and effect within the policy process. From the introduction of direct rule, however, local politicians also became bit players in the political melodrama, no longer the distributors of patronage or largesse, and no longer responsible for the management of budgets or the delivery of services.[11] While the exercise of politics became more equitable after 1972, it simultaneously became less accountable. As political power and responsibility transferred from the political parties to unelected quangos and the Northern Ireland Office,[12] there was a corresponding 'brain drain' within the political class. It became increasingly difficult after 1972 for the parties (especially on the unionist side) to recruit members and activists, with much of the 'talent' seeking alternative avenues for making a positive contribution to their communities, such as through business or voluntary-sector activity. This trend was recognized by the Opsahl Report in 1993 when it commented that

> . . . because of the nature of Northern Irish politics and the democratic deficit in which they are played out, some of the brightest talents have chosen to put their energies into the voluntary sector rather than into formal politics. This further underlines the importance of the voluntary

[11] This remained the case until relatively recently, following the establishment of new institutions resulting from the Good Friday Agreement and the return of devolved responsibilities to Northern Ireland from Westminster.

[12] The branch of the civil service that effectively carries out many of the duties previously discharged by the Stormont government.

> sector and its potential contribution to the search for a settlement and the process of reconstruction that would need to follow it.[13]

Political developments outside Northern Ireland, such as the introduction of the Butler Education Act and the growth of the Welfare State in Britain in the 1940s, had a major impact on political events in Northern Ireland. These reforms, subsequently introduced into Northern Ireland by a reluctant Stormont government, led to a more confident and assertive Catholic population in the 1960s and a larger, better educated Catholic middle class which spearheaded the civil rights movement at the end of that decade. A range of organizations, such as the Campaign for Social Justice (CSJ) formed in 1964, embraced the international language of civil liberties and social justice, partially displacing the old nationalist orthodoxy of single-issue anti-partitionism.[14] The growth of the Catholic middle class was accompanied by pragmatism rather than dogma, and a desire to achieve reform within Northern Ireland rather than to overthrow the state. The explosion of Catholic self-organization in the 1960s, based on international democratic norms such as peaceful direct action, and modelled consciously on the American civil rights movement, posed fundamental problems for the unionist ruling class. In the past, political domination could be justified internally on the grounds of 'national security', the physical threat of militant republicanism and as a consequence of a sullen and abstentionist political representation. Attempts to control peaceful protesters who simply demanded 'British rights for British Citizens' was much more problematic. 'Controlling nationalists who wanted to destroy the state was more ideologically defensible than controlling Catholics who wanted just treatment.'[15] This strategy, of demanding fair treatment and highlighting the structural abuses of the Stormont regime, aided by coverage on the broadcast media of the state's reaction to peaceful protests, led directly to the disintegration of the administration and the introduction of direct rule from Westminster.

[13] A. Pollak, *A Citizen's Inquiry: The Opsahl Report on Northern Ireland* (Dublin: Lilliput Press, 1993), p. 90.

[14] B. O'Leary and J. McGarry, *The Politics of Antagonism* (London: Athlone Press, 1993), p. 160.

[15] Ibid. p. 161.

While nationalist politics metamorphosized in the 1960s, unionist politics were also undergoing a transition, with the introduction of direct rule in 1972 being perhaps the biggest turning point. The absence of an administration at Stormont after 1972 encouraged fracturing to take place within unionist politics and the beginning of a reassessment by the Protestant working class about their alliance with the middle class. In 1969 there was one dominant unionist party, yet by 1973 there were four unionist parties and one independent loyalist party with elected representation. In addition to precipitating the fracture of the unionist electoral monolith, 1972 began a process of philosophical confusion concerning the whole unionist project. Prior to 1972, unionism was relatively easy to understand; it was about preserving the Stormont administration. After the collapse of that administration, however, and the rise in the politically motivated violence that surrounded the period, goals and allegiances within the unionist community started to become more complex. The existence of separate unionist parties all competing for the same vote, encouraged each unionist party to differentiate itself from the others by offering an alternative vision of the future. While some advocated the political integration of Northern Ireland into the United Kingdom in the manner of Scotland or Wales, others called for the restoration of a devolved assembly. At the radical edge, some unionists, disillusioned with their treatment by the British government, argued for the creation of an independent 'Ulster'. The neo-fascist Vanguard Unionist Party was created in 1972, led by William Craig, a former unionist minister in the Stormont government. 'Adopting the fuhreristic leadership style common to such movements in the 1930s, complete with motorcycle outriders, Craig called for the "liquidation" of Ulster's enemies.'[16]

Crucially, with respect to the development of non-governmental organizations (NGOs) and community activism within Protestant politics, the introduction of direct rule in 1972 began the process of revisionism within working-class loyalism and gradually led to a re-evaluation of its relationship with the unionist political élite. Traditionally, the leaders of political unionism were members of a 'squirearchy', which controlled a predominantly working-class move-

[16] Loughlin (1998), p. 60.

ment.[17] This patron-client relationship was often a difficult alliance to maintain, especially during periods of high unemployment. It was accomplished through the mobilization of fear of Irish nationalism. The perpetuation of negative stereotypes concerning Catholic nationalists in Northern Ireland and their potential allies outside the region (not least in the Vatican) fed a political allegiance and cultural identity within unionism that defined itself in contradistinction to nationalists in Northern Ireland. At the same time, the existence of organizations such as the Orange Order served to obscure class differences, promoting the idea that notwithstanding their socio-economic disparities, the Protestant community were blood brothers rather than business partners.

> It perpetuated the notion of a common identity that must be defended in the face of both English and Irish antagonism and propagated the belief that such an identity could be achieved only through group solidarity. By emphasising the tradition of fraternal equality among its members, together with the existence of an external threat, the Orange Order tended to blur class distinctions and helped to reconcile the Protestant working class to the leadership of the landlords and wealthy businessmen.[18]

The introduction of direct rule in 1972 disrupted this relationship within Protestant politics and initiated a period of re-evaluation within working-class loyalism. This was exploited by populist movements such as Ian Paisley's Democratic Unionist Party, which attacked the unionist 'fur coat brigade' for being pompous, remote from the ordinary Ulsterman, and ultimately, for jeopardizing the political, social, economic and religious future of the Protestant community in Northern Ireland. While the nationalist community had never developed a psychological attachment to the Stormont administration or looked to it for political or social leadership, and had consequently developed a tradition of community activism and self-help, this was not the case within unionist politics. The majority of unionists regarded Stormont as *their* government and looked to it for leadership. There was not the same tradition of community

[17] P. Arthur, *Government and Politics of Northern Ireland* (London: Longman, 1987), p. 62.

[18] F. Cochrane, 'The Past in the Present' in P. Mitchell and R. Wilford (eds.), *Politics in Northern Ireland* (Oxford: Westview Press, 1999), p. 11.

organization within the unionist population for the simple fact that for the majority of the time, they had an underdeveloped critique of the political system, a condition reinforced of course, by their perception that the nationalist community was trying to destroy that system. The table below illustrates the manner in which the end of the Stormont administration in 1972 acted as a fulcrum for Catholic/nationalist and Protestant/unionist relationships with the state.

TABLE 6: CHANGING PATTERNS OF COMMUNITY ACTIVISM

Year	*Catholic/Nationalist*	*Protestant/Unionist*
1920–1972	History of community activism	Little history of comunity activism
	Looked inwards for resources and leadership	Looked to the Stormont government for resources and leadership
	Politically fractured	Politically united
	Low community morale	High community morale
1972–	Sense of more equitable political and economic administration	Sense of less fortunate political and economic administration
	Better community morale	Deteriorating community morale
	More united politically	Less united politically
	Growth in community activism	Accelerated growth in community activism

From 1972 therefore, having previously regarded themselves as socially and culturally (if not economically) superior to their Catholic neighbours, the Protestant working class has had to deal with a pervasive sense of failure. They suddenly had to come to terms with the outside world telling them, not that they had built Northern Ireland out of the sweat of their own brows, or as a result of their famed determination, tenacity and fortitude, but rather that they had done so on the back of discrimination and domination of the Catholic community. The following statement from a discussion group held on the Shankill Road in Belfast in 1994 (which was itself a product of unionist working-class community organization) embodies this sentiment:

> There is the belief that over the last twenty-five years the Protestant working class has become increasingly marginalised. Its members feel that their deeply held aspirations have rarely been acknowledged as legitimate by outsiders. Their 'case' has either been denigrated or ignored, or misrepresented by the media and government. . . . Ironically, despite the high profile and vociferousness of many unionist politicians, a frequent complaint from the Protestant working class is a feeling of being 'leaderless'. These politicians may be staunch in defence of the Union, but in the opinion of many working-class Protestants they show little willingness to *lead* their constituents anywhere beyond 'Ulster Says No' and into a new future.[19]

This discussion group went on to suggest that the history of direct rule since 1972, and in particular their experience of British ambivalence to the Union, has been deeply traumatic for the unionist community in Northern Ireland. It was claimed that the actions of the British government since introducing direct rule 'have engendered an increasing sense of betrayal, which twenty-five years on has led to the almost total estrangement of Protestant Ulster from "mother" England. Most working-class loyalists now believe that their "loyalty" counts for little on the mainland (Britain) – Britain no longer wants them.'[20]

One consequence of this sentiment within working-class unionism, has been a desire to provide its own leadership through community activism and self-help initiatives. After 1972 there was no tier of government to look to for leadership, while such leadership as was given, was (until relatively recently) characterized by failure and negativity. Those who saw this felt the need to play 'catch up' with the Catholic community. The history of communal cohesion and self-help within the nationalist community in Northern Ireland since 1920, fuelled by a sense of political and cultural grievance, had acted as a catalyst for that community's development. The Protestant perspective was that they had an underdeveloped sense of community in comparison to their Catholic counterparts. They did not have the same sense of history, were unsure of their culture and were even confused about the meaning of their political allegiance. It was determined that an effort must be made through community development initiatives, to redress this imbalance.

19 Michael Hall *Ulster's Protestant Working Class: A Community Exploration* (Belfast: Island Pamphlet 9, 1994), p. 6.
20 Ibid. p. 7.

> Let's face it – the Republicans have really got their act together, especially their 'Irish' heritage. It has given them a sense of purpose that has sustained them through times of adversity. They've done a thorough job of it, so fair play to them, that's all I can say. But us? Oh no – we stumble from crisis to crisis, and even though we possess an equally legitimate heritage, at times it seems no bloody use to us. It's high time we got *our* act together.[21]

The history of community activism within Protestant working-class areas during the political conflict shows an attempt to get their collective 'act' together.

The economic context

The differential economic development within Catholic and Protestant communities during the Stormont period, and the disruption of unionist economic control following the introduction of direct rule in 1972, are crucial to an understanding of the region's subsequent development, and political attitudes within the two communities. The table below illustrates the differential patterns of economic development within the Catholic and Protestant communities in Northern Ireland before and after 1972.

TABLE 7: DIFFERENTIAL ECONOMIC DEVELOPMENT

	Protestant/Unionist	*Catholic/Nationalist*
1920–1972	Control of local economy	Little economic power
	Good level of eduction	Low qualifications
	Well trained for needs of local economy	Badly trained for needs of local economy
	Good networks	Bad networks
	Dominant stereotype	Inferior stereotype
1972–	Loss of economic control through modernization	Growth in economic power due to greater public sector employment
	Loss of dominant economic position due to reforming legislation	Strengthening economic position due to reforming legislation
	Rising insecurity at loss of economic dominance	Lessening of community alienation due to rise in economic opportunity

[21] Ibid. p. 8.

The economic context is inextricably linked to the prevailing political culture and community perceptions of the 'other' side. From the creation of Northern Ireland in 1920 until the introduction of direct rule in 1972, the Protestant middle class exercised a firm grip on the region's economy. They dominated all aspects of private sector manufacturing industry and finance and also controlled the large public sector firms, as well as being the major influence within agricultural and business organizations. During this period, the Protestant population had better educational qualifications than the majority of Catholics, were better trained for industrial and business occupations, and crucially, were better connected than their Catholic counterparts. In this environment, retaining economic control was facilitated by its self-reproducing character:

> . . . with property, skills, networks of contacts and influence transmitted intrafamilially and therefore intracommunally. The new firms in the 1950s and 1960s sought out the areas with the best infrastructure – in practise Protestant dominated – for economic reasons. . . . Hiring practices typical of the period – taking existing workers' relatives or shop stewards' references, preferring ex-servicemen, advertising first in the immediate neighbourhood, stressing the 'right' attitude to authority – ensured that Protestants rather than Catholics would be hired.[22]

These employment practices were linked, by a process of cultural osmosis, to a stereotyping of the Catholic community as being feckless, untrustworthy, incapable and disloyal, a mindset that was sanctioned at the highest level of the Stormont system. In 1933, Sir Basil Brooke, later to become Prime Minister, encouraged businesses to 'employ good Protestant lads and lassies' on the grounds of national security. 'Roman Catholics were endeavouring to get in everywhere and were out with all their force and might to destroy the power and constitution of Ulster. There was a definite plot to overthrow the vote of Unionists in the North.'[23]

While economic discrimination was not systematic, it was endemic, yet a survey conducted in 1968 found that 74 per cent of Protestant respondents denied that such discrimination existed. The effect on the region's political culture was that many Protestants

[22] J. Ruane and J. Todd, *The Dynamics of Conflict in Northern Ireland* (Cambridge University Press, 1996), p. 153.
[23] Ibid. p. 155.

viewed such complaints with scepticism, and saw them as politically motivated from a nationalist community that was committed to overthrowing the state. For the Catholic population meanwhile, their experience of economic and political exclusion, and the lack of response to their position from the Protestant community, confirmed their belief that they were deliberately being denied basic civil rights and equal access to the levers of economic and political power.

In the wake of the Second World War, the growth of the Welfare State and the British post-war consensus, which accepted state intervention in social policy and economic affairs, the Northern Ireland economy became increasingly dependent on Britain. This trend accelerated after the introduction of direct rule in 1972 as the indigenous and Protestant-controlled private sector continued to decline (especially the traditional industries of shipbuilding, engineering and textiles), while a massive increase took place in public sector expenditure. 'Public sector employment increased from just under 25 per cent of total employment in 1970 to around 39 per cent in 1992; if the employment effects of heavy public expenditure in agriculture and industry are included, the figure is likely to exceed 50 per cent.'[24] While the pattern from the 1970s through the 1980s was for contraction in indigenous family-owned companies and expansion in the public sector, with external investment from Britain and elsewhere, this occurred in an atmosphere of rising unemployment – from 9 per cent in 1979 to 18 per cent in 1986. The political implications of the changing nature of the Northern Ireland economy during this period are obvious. The transition from a dominant locally-owned private sector, to externally-owned businesses and a strong public sector that was no longer controlled by a unionist government at Stormont, dramatically reduced Protestant domination of the economy.

While Protestants remained a significant force at middle-management level within both the public and private sectors, here too their dominance was threatened by Catholic demands for fair employment practices and by legislation introduced by the British government designed to achieve these. After the introduction of direct rule in 1972, the British government appointed a working party to investigate ways of preventing discrimination in private sector employment. The Northern Ireland Constitution Act was a

[24] Ibid. p. 158.

product of the latest political initiative that saw the temporary suspension of direct rule and the return of devolved responsibility in the form of a power-sharing executive; in 1973 it prohibited discrimination on religious or political grounds. In 1976, the Fair Employment Act was passed, which made direct discrimination in public and private employment illegal, while the Fair Employment Agency (FEA) was set up to promote equality of opportunity and to examine individual complaints of abuse. In practical terms, the FEA did little to rectify employment discrimination, but it was regarded by many unionists as being yet another attack on their community and a precursor to affirmative action that would discriminate against the Protestant population. The majority of empirical evidence suggests that there was little change in employment inequality between 1971 and 1985.

> As before Catholics were more likely than Protestants to be unemployed and to experience long-term unemployment: Catholic men were 2.5 times more likely to be unemployed than Protestant men; Catholic women were 1.5 times more likely to be unemployed than Protestant women. The disparity in unemployment rates held for all regions (although there was variation by local area), for every age group, in all the major sectors of the economy, and for men across all social classes.[25]

As public policy has been geared towards redressing the economic inequalities within Northern Ireland, and most legislation (such as the 1989 Fair Employment Act and establishment of the Fair Employment Commission) has been directed at encouraging equality of opportunity, it has been difficult for unionists not to interpret such reforms as an attack upon the Protestant community. Their experience of political and economic reform since 1972, therefore, has largely been a negative one, especially in the context of the monetarist policies pursued by the British government in the 1980s, which resulted in rising levels of unemployment. This has engendered a sense of injustice within working-class Protestant communities, which has become translated into a desire for community activism. This sense of being excluded from economic opportunities is embodied by the following summary of feelings expressed by Protestant community workers at a seminar on Belfast's Shankill Road in 1994:

[25] Ibid. pp. 163–4.

> But what of the social injustices experienced by the Protestant working class? The reality of their daily lives left them little escape from the problems faced by working-class communities anywhere: poorer education, poorer health, more frequent unemployment, a feeling of being dependent, of having limited control over circumstances, a lack of confidence and a squandering of talent. . . . The opinion of many within the Protestant working class is that the adverse socio-economic circumstances confronting them have been ignored by everyone (except when it suits) – the Protestant middle class, the media, the government, the politicians. The remarkable growth of community organizations over the past twenty-five years is a sign that ordinary people realise they have to confront their social and economic circumstances themselves.[26]

Clearly, the development of the NGO sector within Northern Ireland and the emergence of P/CROs after the outbreak of political conflict in 1969, is a consequence of the unique historical, political and economic conditions experienced by the region during the period. The 'democratic deficit', together with the experience of economic deprivation within both Catholic and Protestant working-class areas, led to a growth in community activism, a politicization of people at the 'grass roots' level on socio-economic issues, which in turn provided the infrastructure for P/CROs to develop in response to the political conflict. As the Opsahl Commission reported in 1993: 'In the absence of democratic structures, the powers and influence of the civil service have increased substantially. Many people, who otherwise might join a political party, choose instead to join a community organization or voluntary one.'[27]

The diversity of approaches to the conflict by the P/CROs that evolved out of this democratic deficit, in terms of their analysis of its causes and strategies for its resolution, will be examined in the next chapter.

[26] MIchael Hall (1994), p. 13, 15.
[27] Pollak (1993), p. 13.

4

Attitudes to the Political Conflict in Northern Ireland

This chapter investigates attitudes towards the conflict (and particular matters arising from it) within a range of peace/conflict resolution organizations working within Northern Ireland. It seems reasonable to determine from organizations that are undertaking this type of activity, whether they have ideological views or institutional positions on fundamental questions such as: Why did the conflict start? Why does it continue? How can it be resolved? The purpose here, apart from seeking answers to these questions, is to determine the levels of uniformity or diversity within the P/CRO community in Northern Ireland and to try to account for the differences that exist.

Who started it?

Unsurprisingly, due to the diversity of the organizations involved, attitudes amongst P/CROs concerning the causes of the political conflict in Northern Ireland reflect those of the society at large. There are, however, a number of common themes that reflect not so much a political, as an NGO culture. These centre on the necessity to bring 'ordinary people' and their interpretations and understandings into the political process, and to supplement élite accommodation (and attempts by the political class to reach a historic compromise) with contributions from other sections of civil society.

As with other questions in this study, attitudes to the causes of political instability and inter-ethnic violence are often determined by structural factors. Thus, a cross-community group will invariably possess a different explanatory model to a single-identity community development group. In both cases, the make-up of participants and the focus of activity within the group will often determine the general attitude to questions surrounding the political conflict.

UCAN (Londonderry) provides a classic example of the approach often adopted by single-identity organizations. UCAN was asked about the organization's perception of the nature of the conflict, what it was about, what its sources were and who was responsible for it? UCAN clearly believes that the conflict has originated because there are two very distinct races of people who share the island of Ireland. As one representative bluntly put it: 'There is the British and there is the Irish, and never the twain shall meet.'[1] UCAN did not suggest that both communities were incapable of working together, but stressed that the historic nature of the conflict in Ireland has been one between different races of people. Essentially, therefore, UCAN's view is that the present political conflict in Northern Ireland has centred on 'the British/Irish situation'. In other words, it has been a battle for identity and a power struggle between two groups with conflicting nationality claims.

This is a structural rather than a behavioural analysis, which places less emphasis upon the importance of inter-communal communication than on actions likely to bolster and maintain the Ulster loyalist sense of cultural and political security. UCAN does not underestimate the foundations of the conflict. It is not, for them, a freak of human behaviour that can be resolved if the paramilitaries reform their actions, or if well-intentioned third parties provide enough cross-community seminars, but is instead, 'a war of attrition'.[2] From UCAN's perspective, therefore, the conflict is seen as being part of a war for survival, the survival of the 'Ulster–British' culture, and what they define as their ethnic identity.

> History has shown us, as British people on this island, that we have been pushed from one end of the country to the upper north east corner now, [which is] where the predominant number of Protestants live. It could be seen as a religious thing as well, in that the majority on the island are Roman Catholic, and it's a constant encroachment upon another culture, another identity, and they [Protestants] are being forced and forced and forced to a position [in the north east corner of the island]. Some would say that it is like a latter-day 'Flight of the Earls'.[3]

[1] Representative of UCAN (Londonderry). Interview with authors, 25 February 1997.
[2] Ibid.
[3] Ibid.

Clearly UCAN believes that the Protestant community in Northern Ireland is under siege along all the indices of religion, culture, politics, demography and economics. Much of their analysis seems to flow from a sincerely held belief that their *defined* community is on the retreat along all of these variables. It is this sense of cultural and political insecurity, of being under attack, that produces a desire to fight back, to retrench ground that has been lost or that soon will be. This, of course, is a microcosm of a more general malaise within unionist politics that can be traced from the smallest community group through to the political leadership within the Ulster Unionist Party, together with partner organizations such as the Orange Order.[4]

> [The conflict] is about religious dominance and he who holds the upper hand holds the most land. It is not about sharing anything . . . there are people who talk about sharing and about parity of esteem and equality of treatment.[5]

This clear (if contentious) analysis is not limited to the loyalist community. Dove House Resource Centre is quite similar to UCAN (Londonderry) in terms of articulating a structural analysis of the causes of the political conflict in Northern Ireland, even though they are a single-identity organization from the opposite side of the community, with radically different prescriptions to the resolution of the conflict. When asked for their organizational view of its causes, a representative claimed that Dove House itself did not have a stated policy in relation to the conflict because it was primarily a community development organization focused on social issues of particular importance to the community, such as unemployment, training, care for the elderly and so on. Notwithstanding that fact, the participants in the organization come overwhelmingly from the nationalist/republican side of the community and this fact has inevitably influenced the ethos of the organization. One representative giving a personal opinion, illustrated a fundamentally structural analysis of the conflict:

4 For a detailed analysis of unionist politics see F. Cochrane (ed.), *Unionist Politics and the Politics of Unionism since the Anglo-Irish Agreement*, 2nd edn (Cork University Press, 2001).

5 Representative of UCAN (Londonderry). Interview with authors, 25 February 1997.

> From my own point of view, I would say it's simplistic to say it's all the British Government's fault or it's all the unionists' fault, or it's all the nationalists' fault. I don't think you can look at it in those terms, but what I think is clear, is that there are divisions within this country. Within the six counties in the North here, there are divisions within communities. So I think we must look at what has created those divisions, and once you actually arrive at some definition of it, then you need to remove the causes. . . . Now, in terms of the conflict which erupted in 1969, and what gave rise to that, I think it is clear that if nationalists and Catholics in general, had been treated with a degree of real equality and a degree of respect, then that conflict might never have started. . . . In my opinion the fact that the country is partitioned, leads to those divisions, and those divisions in turn lead to inequality and discrimination, and that in turn leads to conflict and confrontation on the streets.[6]

The UCAN (Londonderry) and Dove House perspectives differ markedly from other human rights groups studied, such as FAIT. While the latter would also emphasize the perceived historical origins of the conflict, they would not view themselves as being the defenders of a specific community or ethnic bloc. When a member of the FAIT management committee was asked to explain the organization's perception of the nature of the conflict, what it was about, whether it was a war or simply 'terrorism' based on common criminality, he declared rather ambiguously, 'It's certainly a war but it's not a just war'.[7] It was suggested that while injustices took place in the past that resulted in the formation of the civil rights movement and rival paramilitary organizations, these injustices (such as being denied employment because of religious affiliation) had largely disappeared, while the paramilitary groups had remained. The reason given to explain why the conflict was still going on, if its causes had largely disappeared, was the control and intimidation exerted by the paramilitary organizations:

> As a result of what happened in 1969, we now have a Mafia, the IRA, UVF, UDA, and these terrorists don't want to lose that. It's very much a power struggle. I mean, the IRA, if you look at their statements, they claim to represent the nationalist people, they claim to be speaking for 'the people of Ireland'. I mean the IRA has something like 5 per cent of the vote of the people in the whole island of Ireland. The methods that

[6] Representative of Dove House Resource Centre. Interview with authors, 17 September 1997.

[7] Representative of FAIT. Interview with authors, 28 November 1996.

> they are using in their own communities are unbelievable; I mean, they're fascists.[8]

While this opinion was expressed with some sincerity, it illustrates the tendency of some P/CROs in Northern Ireland to indulge in emotional analysis driven by the experiences and focus of the organization, rather than an objective assessment of the political environment. When FAIT was asked if it saw the conflict merely in terms of the paramilitaries, or whether it was a wider communal problem with responsibility spreading to other figures within the community in Northern Ireland, the response was that 'middle-class people have a lot to answer for' with regard to the conflict.[9] It was suggested that the middle classes within both communities had a tendency to go home to their leafy suburbs in the evenings and forget about the communal divisions within Northern Ireland. The rather alarming prediction was made that if such a trend continued 'we could have a Bosnia-type situation here'.[10]

These analyses can be classified together as arising out of a pragmatic response to the development of the conflict and its ongoing power and strength. So, single-identity groups such as UCAN (Londonderry) and cross-community, single-issue organizations such as FAIT or the Peace Train, often have an understanding derived from life on the ground related to issues such as community deprivation, ethnic bullying by 'the other side', or simply the actions of 'the terrorists'.

There are other groups within the P/CRO sector who define their approach in a more subtle or complex way, a way that stems directly from their origins, evolution, and the constituencies they try to serve. Quaker House is a good example of a P/CRO which emphasizes a philosophical ethos rather than trying to adapt this to a particular structuralist critique of Northern Ireland's political and historical development. While such contextual factors were important, they were precisely that: the context to the conflict rather than its underlying dynamic cause. One representative from Quaker House commented that 'because of the way Quaker House has been set up

8 Ibid.
9 Ibid.
10 Ibid.

and the things it tries to do, it fits in with a belief that the basis of [conflict resolution] is really to do with trust and the need for people to understand each other and talk to each other. The underlying [cause of the conflict] is the lack of trust between people.'[11] The following remark illustrates the way in which Quaker House regards the political conflict in Northern Ireland as a product of inter-communal sectarianism and destructive social dynamics, rather than an imperfect polity that demands reconstruction to any prescribed design.

> I like the analysis . . . that sectarianism is a pyramid, where you start at the top with the person who is actually throwing the bombs and the bullets, that he or she rests upon someone who is extreme and forever whipping up anger and hatred, and then they rest upon a lot of people who have got a fair amount of prejudice, and they rest on the sort of people . . . who think they are liberal and don't have any views, but in fact they have. So in that sense we are all responsible. It gradually builds. The more extreme views feed on the less extreme ones. [It is] the old dictum you know, that [for an] evil society [to exist] all it requires is for good people to do nothing.[12]

In broad terms it would be possible to describe the P/CRO community in Northern Ireland as being either structuralists or behaviourists with regard to their analysis of the causes of political conflict. In a similar vein to Quaker House, when a representative from Women Together for Peace was asked about the organization's perception of the nature of the conflict, there was a noticeable emphasis upon a behavioural analysis. While it was stressed that politically motivated violence had wider causes than criminality, there was a belief that inter-communal sectarianism could be tackled through communication, contact and schemes for dealing with prejudice, rather than necessitating structural changes to the political regime. 'Women Together think of the conflict as something which each and every one of us has a part in. It is the responsibility of each and every one of us.'[13]

11 Representative of Quaker House. Interview with authors, 14 March 1997.
12 Ibid.
13 Representative Women Together for Peace. Interview with authors, 13 March 1997.

Women Together reject the idea that the conflict is purely the result of the actions of paramilitaries, seeing this as a symptom of a deeper malaise and a product of a much more complex community schism. They argue that it has a lot to do with personal mindsets and that the conflict finds its sustenance because those who do not go so far as to pull the trigger fail to accept a spirit of tolerance and conciliation in their own personal views. As one interviewee succinctly put it: 'Each and every one of us is part of the problem, because we have all created the society we have today.'[14] This perspective is quite common among the more traditional peace and reconciliation groups and risks being seen as encouraging a 'no blame' analysis, where responsibility for the conflict becomes diluted to the point that no one can be held accountable for it.

In the case of Women Together, however (as with many other P/CROs), the fundamental behavioural analysis is tempered by an emphasis on the necessary interaction between structures and behaviour. They accept that the conflict is derived from the region's historical evolution and the sectarianism that these unfinished historical disputes have fostered, which is a structural argument. They add to this the significance of tradition and the problems associated with living in the past, or a mythical version of that past, rather than embracing the future. When asked why people were stuck in the past, the reply was that there has not been an adequate acknowledgement of that past. From this perspective, there needs to be an acknowledgement that injustices occurred in the past; these have to be admitted and got out of the way before society can move on and progress. Women Together believe that there is a collective responsibility on society as a whole for the conflict, and as a consequence they are more interested in restoring relationships than in determining guilt or apportioning blame for past events: 'It is a question of healing, and dealing with the hurt both at a personal and a community level. We have to accept where people are, understand why we are where we are, and start dealing with it and build something new.'[15] Implicit in this view is the need for new inclusive social, community and political structures.

[14] Ibid.
[15] Ibid.

A behavioural analysis is also evident within community development organizations in Northern Ireland such as the Clogher Valley Rural Development Centre. When asked to explain the group's view on the causes of the conflict and the dynamics that fuelled its continuation, a 'contact hypothesis' was proposed. In other words, it was the lack of communication between people of different cultural traditions and political viewpoints that had facilitated and exacerbated stereotypical 'enemy images' of the other.

> I think I would put it down to education, not necessarily education as regards integrated or segregated, although that could play a part in it; . . . I think what the problem is, is that basically you have to have been lucky enough to have [had] the opportunity, through your education or your socialization process, to be able to think for yourself and to have had an opportunity to have met and socialized with other people. . . . I think as far as I'd be concerned, we'd be widely agreed that peoples' perceptions are the problem.[16]

This analysis of the conflict concentrates not on the political, but on community conflict. It believes that through cross-community contact and dialogue, through programmes, projects and courses, the negative stereotypes will break down, and that this is the first step towards achieving inter-communal rapprochement and a resolution of the conflict. Such analysis stresses dysfunctional human relationships as causal factors of sectarianism and conflict, rather than historical forces or malign political structures. The contact hypothesis has come in for sustained criticism in recent years for its assumption, without (or in some cases in spite of) any empirical evidence to support it, that contact between conflict parties will inevitably result in the breaking down of negative stereotypes and a beginning to the process of reconciliation. Stephen Ryan summarizes this point well:

> The crudest version of peace-building is the contact hypothesis, which posits that simply bringing the parties to a conflict together will encourage constructive dialogue and a re-evaluation of negative attitudes. This simplistic view has been convincingly attacked by social psychologists, most notably in a collection of essays edited by M. Hewstone and R. Brown [*Contact and Conflict in Intergroup Encounters,*

[16] Representative of the Clogher Valley Rural Development Centre. Interview with authors, 28 May 1997.

> Oxford, 1986] . . . In fact, many studies have found that attitudes to a host state deteriorate during an extended period of contact.[17]

For P/CROs working *across* the community rather than *within* one particular side, such as the Clogher Valley Rural Development Centre, Women Together and the Ulster People's College, there are difficulties in defining the causes of the conflict. To do so would involve apportioning blame and would therefore run the risk of alienating one half of the community or the other. The Ulster People's College takes a slightly more structural approach than overtly reconciliation P/CROs, but at the same time accepts that inter-communal contact and dialogue is the mechanism by which to address the structural inequalities and inadequacies within the political system. The College recognizes that there is a political problem and that the roots of the conflict lie within a political context. However, it does not consciously define the specific nature of the conflict. This is partly because the causes of the conflict are disputed within the community, and any one definition may lead to a conflict resolution strategy that presupposes a particular outcome or constitutional reform. As one of the College's primary goals is to provide a neutral environment and encourage dialogue between individuals and groups who disagree fundamentally on the causes of the conflict, and therefore on the optimal strategies to resolve it, the College has tended to stand back from taking an explicit position on the nature of the conflict itself. It sees its role not as protagonist with an analysis of the conflict and a particular model to tackle it, but as providing the space and environment within which the actors on both sides of the community can address and, it is hoped, resolve their political and cultural differences. It admitted that it is difficult to avoid de facto linkage between having a definition of the problem and envisaging its solution; however, the College sees its role more in terms of processes than outcomes. The Ulster People's College does, nevertheless, perceive the conflict as being political in a broad sense, and this drives the direction of the organization's community relations and conflict resolution activity. The College believes that part of the reason for the continuation of the political problem is a lack of participation within the community in the political process and the

[17] S. Ryan, 'Transforming Violent Intercommunal Conflict', in K. Rupesinghe (ed.), *Conflict Transformation* (Basingstoke: Macmillan, 1995), pp. 231–2.

'democratic deficit' that existed, until relatively recently, after the introduction of direct rule in 1972.

Perhaps the most interesting organization surveyed with regard to the question concerning the causes of conflict within Northern Ireland is the Committee on the Administration of Justice (CAJ). Responses to questions about the origins and causes of the conflict illustrate the care the organization takes to retain a non-partisan position, while simultaneously operating within possibly the most highly contentious and politicized area of debate, namely policing and the criminal justice system. The group illustrates a classic dilemma for P/CROs in trying to articulate a human rights agenda within a divided society without stepping over the line and adopting a position of political advocacy.

The general approach of the CAJ is to claim that abuses of human rights by agencies of the state within a context of bad emergency law and an inefficient criminal justice system, have contributed to the conflict rather than helped to address or resolve it. Following from this, any attempt to engage in a conflict resolution strategy must, by definition, have as a goal the creation of a society where everyone is treated fairly and accorded rights and justice on the basis of equality. Consequently, therefore, in the analysis of the CAJ, issues of justice and fairness are at the heart of the conflict and provide the dynamic for its perpetuation. At the same time as advocating a human rights agenda, the group maintains that it has no overt political prescriptions, that is, views on the constitutional reform of Northern Ireland. It believes simply that whoever is responsible for the region (whether the government rests within Great Britain or the Republic of Ireland) needs to respect and protect the human rights of the citizens.

> So those are, if you like, the defining elements. The other bit of that would be a strong sense that violence is unacceptable and has no part to play in building a lasting peace, and those two things together – no position on the constitutional question and strong opposition to the use of violence – are important parts. That, plus the sense that the issue of human rights has a part to play, would really sum up the Committee's thinking on the conflict.[18]

For P/CROs who adopt a service delivery as well as a campaigning side to their activities (as the CAJ does), the issue of defining the

[18] Representative of the CAJ. Interview with authors, 6 June 1997.

conflict is a very practical one. Such P/CROs attempt to look in two directions at once by, on the one hand, confronting what they regard as abuses of human rights by the state and its agencies, and on the other, trying to lobby for changes to the government's criminal justice system. As their focus is mainly on the legislative inadequacies and executive abuses of the state's role in the conflict, it has to find a way of addressing such issues without looking as if it is attacking the state for political reasons, because this would inevitably politicize the organization, alienate one section of the community, and thus limit its ability to operate effectively.

With this dilemma in mind, it was suggested to the organization that there might be a difference between adopting a position on a particular constitutional outcome and having an analysis of the causes of the conflict. Did the CAJ simply ignore, or avoid, developing a position on the actual roots of the conflict because this might diminish its ability to deal with the consequences of the conflict? Would the development and public presentation of any such analysis of the causes of the conflict reduce the access of the organization within one or both of the main communities in Northern Ireland, and possibly the British government, thus inhibiting its effort to highlight human rights abuses? The following statement from a representative of the CAJ suggested that such a pragmatic perspective did indeed operate in relation to this question:

> Well it seems to me that an analysis of the roots of the conflict, the particular roots which you identify, place you on the political spectrum, regardless of whether or not you then adopt a particular constitutional settlement, so we wouldn't engage in an exercise of trying to say these are what the roots of the conflict are. What we are saying very clearly, is that abuses of people's rights are part of the conflict and feed and fuel the conflict and that, historically, issues of fairness and people's own sense of fairness, have been central to the conflict, and if you want to do something about it then you need to address that. That's as far as we would go. I mean the Committee is deliberately and very consciously not taking a position on a whole series of issues, and the reason why it's not taking a position on that whole series of issues is because if it were to do so, it would inhibit its ability to be effective on the issues which it wants to work on.[19]

Although groups will talk generally in discussions about the nature of the conflict, there is a reluctance to place much emphasis on their

[19] Ibid.

approach to it. This is more pronounced in cross-community organizations, but is to be found in community development, human rights and reconciliation groups as well. For example, a representative from the Springfield Inter-Community Development Project claimed that while there was an organizational view that the conflict was between two communities over nationality and territory, it was important not to blame either side for it, but to seek ways whereby it could be positively addressed. 'There needs to be inclusive dialogue to actually discuss [the conflict]. But in terms of blaming . . . we wouldn't actually reinforce that in any sense, but we would say it's more how we deal with it, rather than who we blame.'[20] It was suggested that it was the nature of society that perpetuated the political conflict, rather than simply the individuals who engaged in paramilitary activity. The resemblance to other P/CROs examined, such as Quaker House and Women Together, is clear, as the causes of conflict are envisaged in an amorphous way to include the society as a whole, rather than crystallized down to a specific section of the community.

> Whether people went out and joined paramilitary groups, or whether they sat in the house, they were guilty, I suppose, by their silence, as well as being guilty by particular actions. . . . Some people have actually acted on the sidelines as some sort of cheerleaders for the paramilitaries, never actually spoke to them, or soiled their hands, or got involved in it. So they're just as responsible [for the conflict]. . . . So our attitude is that there's nobody who's wholly innocent and nobody who's wholly guilty.[21]

Once again this response emphasizes the present and future rather than the past. There is a clear effort to concentrate on how to move out of the conflict, rather than to come to any definitive conclusion as to why it exists or what its underlying causes are. However, it again poses the question as to whether P/CROs can actually contribute to resolving a conflict if they consciously avoid an organizational view as to its causes and dynamic forces?

There is an obvious practical advantage to be gained for many of these P/CROs (especially those with a cross-community orientation) in not 'nailing their colours to the mast', as to do so might alienate

[20] Representative of the Springfield Inter-Community Development Project. Interview with authors, 13 August 1997.

[21] Ibid.

potential supporters and thereby reduce their effectiveness. However, the price for such pragmatism is analytical incoherence, together with a 'no blame' culture that tends to obscure rather than enlighten.

Peace plans: P/CRO views on resolving the conflict

There is a very distinct non-governmental ethos that runs throughout the P/CRO sector in Northern Ireland, from the single-identity community development groups to the cross-community reconciliation organizations. There was a sense that the formal political process, and the actors within it, had failed (up until the Good Friday Agreement of April 1998) to produce a viable political settlement and had excluded the 'ordinary people' from exerting their influence. The attitude of many groups is governed by a desire to see a broadening of political dialogue and an inclusion of civil society within the debate. However, beyond this general theme, attitudes towards conflict resolution strategies are often determined by the structural requirements of the P/CRO, the focus of its activity and the nature of its constituency. For example, a strong anti-elitist thread runs through UCAN (Londonderry) thinking, which is a direct consequence of the group's composition. It is a working-class organization and reflects working-class attitudes and values. UCAN places little faith in the political élites, believing strongly that politicians do not work for the ordinary people, but for themselves and the narrow vested interests of their own political organizations.

> The situation, the way UCAN would see it, would be that we are here to give voice to those whom the politicians have yet to give voice to. The ordinary working-class people on the ground, who yes, admit that they are Protestants, but they are Protestants in such a way that they see they can share this city [Londonderry], they can share this island, they can live side by side with others of different traditions, or religions, or cultures irrespective of who they are, and that there is a place for everyone. And it is a matter of making our voice heard and trying to promote an understanding in others of other ethnic origins, of what our culture is, what our identity is, and see if we can change their prejudice about us and vice versa, by mutual dialogue or discussion.[22]

Economic and social regeneration also plays a key role in UCAN's conflict resolution strategy. The group believes that the material

[22] Representative of UCAN (Londonderry). Interview with authors, 25 February 1997.

circumstances of working-class Protestants must be improved if that section of the community (which is essentially the constituency from which Protestant paramilitaries are drawn) is to become interested in, or amenable to, a reconciliation agenda. This is sometimes referred to as 'capacity building', the idea being that the capacity for anti-sectarian work can be built within a community before it begins to interact with those outside of the identity group. A UCAN spokesperson claimed that people tended to make ill-informed choices when they did not have the information available to them, a tendency demonstrated in 1996 by the attitude to contentious Orange parades in Londonderry, and the demonstrations in the city commemorating 'Bloody Sunday' (when fourteen Catholics were killed by the British Army on 30 January 1972). In both instances politicians took a stand and people came onto the streets. UCAN (Londonderry) believes that the 'ordinary people' have been, and continue to be, the victims of mass manipulation by the political élites. It was claimed that the nature of political culture in Northern Ireland was such that if an individual decided not to follow their tribal bandwagon, then he or she was likely to be condemned as a traitor to their community and thereafter would find it very difficult to exist within that community. UCAN believes that on both sides of the community the parameters of debate have become too narrow and are too strictly defined by the political leaders of unionism and nationalism. As a consequence, people find it hard to step outside these boundaries and therefore difficult to engage in the sort of progressive political thinking that might contribute to a resolution of the political conflict. UCAN believed that there needed to be an empowerment of the grass roots through dialogue and communication. From this perspective, when documents such as the North Report (government-appointed body on contentious Orange parades) are commissioned, they should be brought down to the grass roots level for consultation within both sections of the community in Northern Ireland, to explain what their purpose, intent and objectives are, so that these communities could feel some sense of ownership and participation in the political process. '[They need to say] "Right, this is why we are doing this. Where would you like the changes, what needs to happen here? Can you accept this?"'[23] It was

[23] Ibid.

claimed that if such contacts were not established, people would be left in a position of ignorance and become disillusioned with the political process, seeing it as being remote from their lives and sphere of influence. The Anglo-Irish Agreement was cited as an example, as it was imposed over the heads of the ordinary Protestant population in November 1985, increasing fear and confusion, and resulting in a negative political reaction. Critics of this view might point out, of course, that the Anglo-Irish Agreement was the product (rather than the cause) of negativity within unionist politics. Nevertheless, UCAN's concern with consultation between the political élites and the people they claim to represent reflects a broader NGO ethos that emphasizes inclusiveness and transparency within peace processes. This theme has been developed further by academics such as John Paul Lederach, who frames it in terms of 'building a peace constituency' through 'indigenous empowerment':

> Empowerment is the procedural element of validating and providing space for proactive involvement in conflict transformation. . . . Building a community of people is as important as the program. That people should see themselves as resources working on their own problems matters at least as much as any given product or solution. The principle of indigenous empowerment suggests that conflict transformation must actively envision, include, respect, and promote the human and cultural resources from within a given setting.[24]

Perspectives within single-issue human rights groups on developing conflict resolution strategies tend to be more generalized, perhaps because their analysis of the causes of conflict are less evolved than many single identity groups or broader-based human rights organizations. FAIT's approach to resolving the conflict, for example, is tied into their very specific focus on paramilitary punishment attacks: 'The only way we can move forward is to get rid of the paramilitaries, or to convince the paramilitaries that they don't get anywhere with violence. That violence begets violence.'[25] A representative from FAIT was asked if the organization favoured any particular political model, or would criticize political parties for their ideas if they conflicted

[24] J. P. Lederach, 'Conflict Transformation in Protracted Internal Conflict: The Case for a Comparative Framework', in Rupesinghe (1995), pp. 212–13.

[25] Representative of FAIT. Interview with authors, 14 March 1997.

with the ethos of the group. Speaking before the Good Friday Agreement was reached in April 1998, this interviewee was critical of the political élites, yet the analysis of how the conflict should be tackled was generalized and vague: 'FAIT are non-political but I would criticize the DUP for their attitude, I would criticize the SDLP for not moving . . . and the same applies to the Official Unionists [sic] as well. [FAIT would favour] Reconciliation. I mean it's the only way to solve any conflict isn't it? Let's get together and put all our fears and everything else onto the table and reconcile our differences.'[26]

The effort to resolve the political conflict by building cross-community reconciliation is fundamental to P/CROs that take a behavioural rather than structural approach to conflict resolution in Northern Ireland. One of the clearest advocates of this strategy is Women Together, who believe that the conflict will only be resolved when people change existing mindsets that allow the violence to persist, and become committed to accepting collective responsibility for it. 'We feel that it has a lot to do with finding the starting point, and the starting point is acceptance that there are two main traditions in Northern Ireland and that they deserve equal respect.'[27] The main focus of Women Together, therefore, is on attitudinal change, as they see everything else flowing from this in terms of political and social reform. Once a culture of tolerance and respect for the opposing viewpoint becomes accepted within Northern Ireland, then the group sees the possibility of an end to politically motivated violence and a chance for progressive change to take place within society. It is argued within reconciliation groups such as Women Together, that the resolution of the political conflict will not occur overnight as there is 'a lot of hurt' within society that will take time to heal. However, they see the first step as a recognition and acknowledgement that the hurt exists, and a collective apology within society for the violence and injustice that has taken place. 'There are a lot of apologies to be made for what happened, and that includes [the British] government as well as the paramilitary organizations.'[28] While Women Together is a P/CRO that has worked to reduce

[26] Ibid.

[27] Representative of Women Together for Peace. Interview with authors, 13 March 1997.

[28] Ibid.

community conflict throughout the period colloquially known as 'the troubles', there is a danger that it approaches the issue of conflict resolution in the manner that a therapist approaches a patient. Those who adhere to a more structural analysis of the political conflict in Northern Ireland are unlikely to be attracted by mutual apologies, or by efforts to reduce sectarianism through 'group hugs', metaphorical or literal.

While Woman Together could be seen as the antithesis of a single-identity organization, with its stress on cross-community dialogue and its primarily behavioural analysis of the conflict, it displays a similar anti-elitist ethos to some single-identity groups such as UCAN (Londonderry). 'It is very important that all levels of society are involved in the solution to this conflict, and that's the people from the grass roots up. They need to be working together, they need to be working on [the] reconciliation of those communities whilst the politicians are doing their bit.'[29]

The case of Women Together is an interesting example of the dilemma facing a cross-community reconciliation organization. Clearly, there is a lot of debate within groups such as Women Together about how they should approach issues relating directly to the political conflict. One of the central issues determining Women Together's conflict resolution strategy concerns the extent of its involvement in contentious political issues, such as public demonstrations and pickets, and the potential for such activity to damage the credibility of the organization. Conversely, if the organization is too conservative its credibility will also be damaged, Women Together being seen as irrelevant to the major political disputes that are causing division and sectarianism within society. Clearly, therefore, a narrow line exists between doing too much and doing too little. This is often complicated by organizational changes within P/CROs over time. For example, the structure of Women Together has changed from being a collection of autonomous locally-based groups into a more centralized organization. This in turn has produced debate and discussion amongst the membership over the group's activities and ideological focus. It was suggested by one representative of the organization that the older members still hankered after the previous form of direct action, where small local groups would be formed within

[29] Ibid.

interface areas and would challenge specific instances of sectarian conflict. The more recent strategy is based on less localized and more large-scale activities using the media and general public mobilization. It was pointed out that the group's attitude to conflict resolution in Northern Ireland was intrinsically linked to their specific organizational evolution.

> It is a big debate. Because the newer members that are coming in now weren't there twenty years ago. Society's changed and there's much more for women to do outside now, there are many more opportunities for leisure and that sort of thing. Whereas when they came together in the early days, whilst there was a strong voice against violence, they also came together for social interaction. . . . To get together as friends . . . to take them[selves] out of the house, and they [devised] social activities that they could do together, as well as the other side of it. But I think the mass of members do believe that it is mindsets that have to change.
>
> . . . We have always stuck to the idea that it has to start with the individual. You have to look at yourself, look at the sectarianism within yourself and ask yourself some serious questions and try and work on yourself first. And this organization helps you do that. And only then can you work with your family and your community.[30]

The attitude of Women Together is similar in nature to those of other P/CROs within Northern Ireland with a cross-community ethos. There is a strong emphasis on the need to maximize dialogue; a belief that wider society rather than just the paramilitary groups is responsible for the continuation of violence; that there is a role for civil society to complement the activity of the political actors; and that they are political with a small 'p'. The Ulster People's College, for example, is a P/CRO that exhibits many of these features. In general terms the College has no explicit position on how the conflict should be resolved. More precisely, the organization has no formal model of government that it advocates as a compromise settlement between the two dominant blocs of unionism and nationalism in Northern Ireland. However, it would be accurate to say that the College (at least until the return of devolved powers following the Good Friday Agreement) believed that the political structures pre-Agreement had failed the people of Northern Ireland and that a new set of political relationships had to be constructed with which all could identify.

[30] Ibid.

Perhaps as a consequence of its professional interest in the issue, the College does have a well-defined and coherent approach to the resolution of the conflict. This is based not on *outcomes* but upon *processes*. Central to the College's approach, is the view that the political culture and political dialogue must become more mature and rational; that opportunities for dialogue and debate between the political actors must be maximized; and that the whole process of politics must become less elitist, more inclusive, and involve a greater section of society. While the College does not advocate a particular political model, or position itself at some point on the nationalist/unionist axis, it has developed a range of ideas on issues surrounding justice, human rights, citizenship, democracy, social inclusion and equality, and regards these as a central part of the dynamic which will eventually lead to the transformation of the political conflict and some form of reconciliation between divided communities. As a consequence, instead of adjudicating upon the validity of the political ideas or policy statements that emerge from the political parties along traditional nationalist or unionist lines, the College tests these policies against their own set of values concerning justice, democratic citizenship and so on. The attitude of the College to any policy will therefore depend upon the extent to which it satisfies these criteria, rather than whether it furthers or diminishes a specific ideological objective.

The carefully defined approach taken by the Ulster People's College contrasts rather sharply with single-issue P/CROs such as the Peace Train organization, which tended to take a much more ad hoc view of the wider political context. The emphasis here was on a single-issue concern with paramilitary violence. This was partly due to the fact that the Peace Train was a coalition of participants from a range of political parties who would have found it difficult to reach agreement on a wider political agenda. In common with other P/CROs in Northern Ireland that favoured behavioural interpretations of the conflict, the Peace Train took the view that the provision of cross-community contact was 'a good thing', and would assist the breaking-down of sectarian stereotypes that fuelled political violence. 'I think there was a somewhat diffuse view that the Peace Train offered an opportunity for Catholics and Protestants, Northerners and Southerners, to come together and meet and [that] that was a good thing, that kind of direct meeting and acquaintanceship is important in terms of breaking down barriers and suspicion and so on. I think that's probably as far as it went.'[31]

The attitude of the Springfield Inter-Community Development Project to the resolution of the political conflict in Northern Ireland once again illustrates the way in which structural factors (in this case the group's position as an inter-community development group), play a large part in determining the organizational view. When asked whether the best approach lay in building trust through dialogue between the two communities, or alternatively, as single-identity groups suggested, providing resources for those communities as a precursor to cross-community contact, a representative of the organization suggested a third option. This was that, rather than attempting to achieve trust between communities within interface areas where sectarian feelings were high, a more realistic goal was to create an understanding between the two communities and a sense of empathy within unionist and nationalist working-class areas that their socio-economic circumstances were the same. Beyond this, like so many other P/CROs working in Northern Ireland, the Springfield Project had no organizational view on the resolution of the conflict:

> I think our argument is that, if you leave the constitutional position aside, we believe that we need to deal with the reality of the situation. The reality of the situation is that we live in Northern Ireland, which is within the United Kingdom, the British Government controlling the Exchequer, they lift the taxes and they control our education, our housing, our economic life for all of that. That's what we have to be making sure, that groups are actually getting what they should be getting, out of that. Now, in a sense, if the work that we are doing is preparing the ground in terms of allowing people to come together to look at the real political situation, then that's okay, but it's not our job to turn unionists into nationalists or to turn nationalists into unionists. It's our job to lay in front of people the facts, and the hard facts of socio-economic life in Northern Ireland. It's also our job to say to people, if people were doing A, B and C together, that maybe D, E and F could be achieved.[32]

The Springfield Project's Operational Plan for 1996–99 provides an indication of its approach to conflict resolution activity: 'Everyone affected by a particular conflict needs to be involved in movement

[31] Representative of the Peace Train. Interview with authors, 5 August 1997.
[32] Representative of the Springfield Inter-Community Development Project. Interview with authors, 13 August 1997.

towards its resolution.'[33] This provides an indication of the way in which the Project saw paramilitary organizations fitting into a conflict resolution strategy, and illustrates a difference from other P/CROs within Northern Ireland such as FAIT and the Peace Train that advocated a policy of confrontation and marginalization of those involved in politically motivated violence. Once again, the viewpoint of the P/CRO towards the conflict is organically linked to the social profile of the people involved in running the Springfield Project and the type of community development work they are involved in.

> We would argue that an understanding of those who engage in armed struggle, or of the organizations which sustain them, is not, and cannot be, adequately represented by simplistic sloganizing or labelling borne from anger or frustration. . . . A recognition that those engaged in violent struggle also have a contribution to make, perhaps the major contribution, does not in any way detract from justifiable anger at the consequences of their actions nor may it help in easing the pain felt by the victims of all violence or the hurt endured by their families and friends.
>
> . . . Such a recognition, however, may be the first step toward ending our violence, giving some sense of meaning to the sacrifice and pain endured by all our people, and creating positive movement from 25 years of hurting.[34]

In a similar fashion to UCAN (Londonderry), the single-identity organization Dove House Resource Centre favoured a structural rather than behavioural approach to resolving the political conflict. When a representative was asked whether the group would advocate a breaking down of the two main communal blocs in Northern Ireland via a programme of reconciliation, or the perpetuation of these blocs through an accommodation of the existing political élites, it was clear that fundamental political change was seen as necessary rather than the 'change in mindsets' approach favoured by reconciliation groups such as Women Together or the Peace Train.

> Well, Dove House takes a pragmatic view on those issues. Dove House believes that there should be cooperation between Dove House as an organization, and other community groups, whether those other groups

[33] Springfield Inter-Community Development Project. Operational Plan 1996–99.

[34] Ibid.

> are based in a unionist area or in a nationalist area, and that has been the case, where there has been joint cooperation with other groups. But Dove House hasn't discussed this issue in terms of, 'This will resolve the political conflict in this country'. I personally would have the view that that type of activity [reconciliation and communication] won't resolve the political conflict. You must resolve the issues that give rise to the conflict before you can even hope to break down those barriers. Now that's not to say that you don't continue on the ground, in terms of that contact and that co-operation, because there are times when it can be useful in terms of lessening tension, avoiding confrontation, assisting the process of reconciliation, but I don't believe that they in themselves will actually resolve the conflict.[35]

While the dynamics of P/CROs such as Dove House and UCAN (Londonderry) were very similar in terms of their having a structural analysis of the conflict, and their desire to represent and work on behalf of specific ethnic and geographical constituencies, this did not produce any discernible meeting of minds. Despite their geographical proximity to one another, their diametrically opposed structural analyses of the conflict ensured that there was a complete absence of overlapping memberships between the organizations. This, in a sense, was a microcosm of Northern Ireland society as a whole: communities that live together cheek-by-jowl, yet seem at the same time to be fundamentally separate. Because such organizations define the Northern Ireland situation in structural terms, and because this is closely associated with a political or historical analysis, or a 'zero sum' game, the central issue for them is the constitutional one, even when much of their ideological analysis is shared and many of the problems facing their constituencies are common to both.

P/CROs and the Northern Ireland conflict: Some conclusions

While many current practitioners claim to be above this argument, there remain two fundamental approaches to conflict resolution work that can be seen from the evidence provided in this chapter. One sees communication and dialogue between the rival factions as being intrinsically worthwhile. This could involve the provision of a neutral venue for a community discussion on a contentious political

[35] Representative of Dove House Resource Centre. Interview with authors, 17 September 1997.

issue, or activities that bring these factions together on a non-political basis. The underlying assumption here is that communication between individuals in a non-threatening environment breaks down negative stereotypes and assists understanding between those who differ fundamentally in their political opinions.

Many people who advocate the community development approach, regard this sort of activity as essentially ephemeral, touching on the symptoms of the conflict but failing to address its fundamental causes. The Springfield Inter-Community Development Project, for example, as explained above, was formed out of frustration with the type of community relations activity that had been going on in the area up to that point. A lot of work had been done with young people in this area of Belfast, taking them out of their environment on holidays, into situations where they would meet people from 'the other side'. However, when they came back home, their sectarian attitudes and behaviour soon re-emerged because the environment and culture around them was stronger than any experience they had had during their holiday. While they were changed for the time they were away and made friends, they reverted quickly after their return because, as one person graphically put it, 'It was still a question of Orangies or Taigs'.[36]

The alternative approach, attempted by community development groups such as the Springfield Project, was to try to effect change from within urban interface areas by involving the parties to the conflict. Thus, instead of trying to marginalize paramilitary organizations by reducing support from within the community for their actions, as FAIT and the Peace Train advocated, an effort was made to engage with and involve the paramilitaries, to demonstrate that inter-community work was not a threat to them, but was actually contributing to the advancement of the communities they were members of and claimed to be representing and defending.

This, in essence, was the thinking behind the peace process on a wider level and lies at the heart of the Good Friday Agreement: provide an inclusive dialogue between the parties to the conflict and design political structures that all sides can buy into and feel ownership of. Critics of this approach (some of whom would also be

[36] Representative of the Springfield Inter-Community Development Project. Interview with authors, 13 August 1997.

anti-Agreement) suggest that this is an impractical/immoral strategy, as it fails to lay 'blame' at the door of the 'perpetrators' of violence, panders to their demands, and makes the whole political process dependent upon their support.

There are three main approaches favoured by these community development organizations. One approach is to pursue community development work on a *cross-community* basis as practised, for example, by the Clogher Valley Rural Development Centre. A second strategy, as represented by the Springfield Project, is to engage in community development on an *inter-community* basis, working separately with both sides of the community on the basis of their common socio-economic interests. The third alternative is *single-identity* activity, where the community group will work with one specific section of the population. The examples of the single-identity approach examined above are Dove House Resource Centre and UCAN (Londonderry). The main focus of such groups is to redress economic and social deprivation within their own pre-defined community, as a first step towards decreasing sectarianism or tackling more contentious political or cultural issues. There is a major question here, of course, as to where the internal capacity-building of such groups stops and the cross-community element begins? Are such organizations simply trying to access funding opportunities rather than address the conflict? Is this work merely an exercise in resource acquisition for their own communities, rather than being part of a conflict resolution strategy, and is this simply producing 'better educated bigots?' (See Chapter 7 for a more detailed analysis of the impact of single-identity P/CROs on conflict resolution in Northern Ireland.)

When single-identity groups are asked why they do not pursue cross-community activities, they reply that within interface areas it is not realistic for them to try to engage in cross-community reconciliation until their own communities are built up to the point that they are capable of participating in dialogue with those beyond their own community. A representative from UCAN remarked that if he asked some of the young people in his area to enter a debate with their Catholic counterparts in the neighbouring district, they would simply refuse to do so.

Perhaps the most ironic finding from the evidence presented in this chapter, is that within the P/CRO sector in Northern Ireland, there is a very underdeveloped analysis of the causes of the conflict, and possible scenarios for its resolution. At first glance this is odd; these organizations seek to engage in conflict resolution yet they do not (for the most part) have a very closely defined sense of why that conflict exists, other than in the most primitive of terms, i.e., that it is a product of the region's dysfunctional historical evolution, or due to our behavioural inability to communicate positively with one another.

There is an explanation for this apparent myopia. Many of those people drawn to peace/conflict resolution organizations are motivated by the symptoms of the conflict which, of course, are real, tangible and terrible, rather than the causes of that conflict which may be political, historical and invisible. As it is the effects of the conflict rather than its underlying causes that impact on people in their everyday lives, it is understandable that they will mobilize around these, whether that involves campaigning against the use of plastic bullets (CAJ and Dove House), the bombing of the Belfast–Dublin railway line (the Peace Train), or paramilitary punishment beatings (FAIT). It is also the case, of course, that the effects of the conflict are much easier to tackle than the causes, as they are often more visual and self-contained. As a consequence, the goals and objectives of many peace/reconciliation organizations revolve around the effects of the conflict, or, put another way, the human costs of the conflict. In an attempt to gain support for these goals, the group will normally attempt to attract as wide a constituency as possible. It will often try to appear non-partisan, non-political or apolitical. It may consciously seek to include Protestant, Catholic and Dissenter, unionist and nationalist, loyalist and republican, in its membership or even on its management committee. This will often be quite a natural process, and it would be rare that such selection operated on an overtly artificial basis. Nevertheless, everyone can count silently and there is often an unconscious understanding within P/CROs that it is important to maintain a balance in participation. While this concern with ethnic balance is often subtle and unspoken, there have been more overt instances where it has been funding-driven. While few P/CROs would admit it, recruiting a few 'token Taigs' or 'token Prods' onto the management committee rarely does any damage in the constant search for funding and resources.

The combined effect of the heterogeneous composition of many peace/conflict resolution groups, and their concentration on the symptoms of the conflict, is that they are constrained within certain limitations, often willingly of course. To move away from the central focus of the organization, or to attempt to broaden that focus by moving from the specific to the general, often leads to internal animosities, fractures and splits in the group, with some people effectively saying 'That's not what I signed up for'. This is often more of a problem, of course, for single-issue groups which begin with a very narrow focus, such as the Peace Train, rather than organizations like the Peace People or the Corrymeela community, who incorporate a broader perspective.

It is often the case in Northern Ireland that the desire to broaden the coalition of support for the organization precludes it from adopting a developed critique of the existing political order or any broader analysis of the roots of the conflict. Thus, instead of addressing causes they address symptoms, whether these be the concern of the CAJ with an inadequate criminal justice system, FAIT's attempt to stop paramilitary punishment attacks, or the Peace Train's campaign to stop the bombing of a railway line. Within many of the P/CROs involved in conflict resolution activity in Northern Ireland, most of the analysis of the causes of the conflict is kept at the general level. Statements such as 'we have all suffered from the conflict' abound. While this may be the result of a desire not to alienate potential supporters, it often results in the P/CRO sector as a whole appearing bland, middle-of-the-road . . . nice. Consequently, such groups have often been criticized for being irrelevant to and remote from, those at the sharp end of community sectarianism and the political conflict.

5

Peace People: A Profile of the P/CRO Activist

Who are the people that devote their energies to peace and conflict resolution activity and why do they bother? It is not everyone who feels compelled to give up their time and energy to become involved in the activities of P/CRO organizations, often at great personal cost in terms of physical or verbal attack from oppositional groups. Clearly, few people do it for the money! This chapter will illustrate the relationship between these individuals and the P/CROs they become involved in and will look at why they join, why they leave, and what is expected of them.

Once again, as with other issues covered in the book, the origins and focus of the organization can often determine the profile of participants. A reconciliation group, for example, is likely to have people involved who espouse moderate political opinions, and few activists who adopt radical or exclusivist positions. Similarly, a community development organization will attract people with specific social and cohesive interests, in a way that a broad-based reconciliation group will not. This chapter will demonstrate that the P/CRO sector is infused with the NGO culture from which it emerged.

The motivating factors for involvement include a belief in community rather than individualism; a concern to work for the betterment of that perceived community (and as the narrative will demonstrate, 'community' is defined in different ways by different people); a sense of a moral imperative to make a positive contribution to that defined community; an optimism that such activity will 'make a difference'; the strength of personality to run an organization on very limited resources and often against opposition from one (or both) of the main communities in Northern Ireland; a set of moral values taken from the NGO sector which provide many P/CROs with an organizational ethos based on concepts such as non-violence, citizenship, dialogic democracy, pluralism, multiculturalism and partnership. Often these values will be stronger within the group than the political issues to which such concepts are applied.

Political and social characteristics

When a representative from the loyalist single-identity P/CRO, UCAN (Londonderry), was asked to describe the typical activist, the value system outlined above was clearly expressed. The response demonstrated not only the strong sense of community, but also that belief common to many single-identity organizations, that their defined community is under attack. Participants, it was claimed, were working-class people who were very concerned about their community, felt aggrieved that the statutory bodies had let them down, and wanted to do something about it. '. . . You have a real feeling, a real belonging to your community and want to help, want to make things better for your community.'[1] While UCAN is an overwhelmingly Protestant organization, this defines a political and ethnic, rather than a theological, group of people. 'Nobody ever mentions religion. We feel honestly, while we are all religious, none of us have a lot of respect for [institutionalized] religion. We feel that the Church has let us down.'[2]

The social and political profile of UCAN is that participation is geographically specific, coming mainly from the Waterside area of Londonderry. It is a single-identity organization with activists coming exclusively from the Protestant side of the community. While it is claimed that politics plays a negligible part in the group's ideological focus or activities, it is clear that a unionist ethos is fundamental to those who become involved, encouraged perhaps by the core organizational goal of articulating, promoting and defending the 'Ulster–British culture' within Northern Ireland.

At the same time, it is clear that the socio-economic issues that concern UCAN (Londonderry) tend to have a big influence upon the

1 Representative of UCAN (Londonderry). Interview with authors, 10 March 1997.
2 Ibid.

type of people who are attracted to the organization. As the following explanation by a representative of UCAN illustrates, those who become involved feel that working-class Protestants in Derry have all suffered a similar experience of deprivation. There is an unambiguous sense of abandonment by other sections of society and of decline within the defined community (in this case working-class Protestants), and a feeling of moral obligation to arrest, or at least identify such decline.

> The working-class people are the ones who are always left with the problems. When people live in this area and get educated, they move out and that's a problem. We reckon that's because, first of all, the Churches haven't recognized the deprivation that is there, they skip over it with this glossy religious thing. The middle-class people don't want to know and it is always the working-class people who actually see the problems and are actually facing the problems. I could quite easily walk away from this. My wife's a schoolteacher, we've enough money, but I see the problems and it's not fair on the young people. But truly it's because we're left in the middle of it, everybody else has walked away and wiped their hands of it.[3]

Like UCAN and many other single-identity groups in Northern Ireland, Dove House Resource Centre is also a very cohesive body. The organization's catchment area, which centres on the Bogside and Brandywell areas in Derry, is also the region from which most of the participants of the group come. Those involved are predominantly working class. The political affiliation of activists is almost universally on the republican/nationalist side of the community, with a tendency towards the former. There is a good gender balance, with women outnumbering men on some occasions on the management committee. Most of the participants are Catholics, though there is a wide variety of theological commitment from conservatives to non-practising Catholics. In a similar vein to the pattern of participation in UCAN (Londonderry), most of the key activists have a history of involvement within their community on social issues such as poverty and unemployment. Likewise, the political affiliations of participants are almost exclusively left-of-centre, with a heavy socialist influence permeating the group.

The participant profile of single-identity organizations like Dove House and UCAN (Londonderry) contrasts sharply with that of

[3] Ibid. 15 April 1997.

single-issue human rights groups such as FAIT. FAIT is composed of activists from both religious communities and both sides of the unionist/nationalist political argument. There is no significant representation of political radicalism in the organization in relation to republican and loyalist opinion; most of those involved are either non-aligned politically, or supporters of the 'moderate'[4] Alliance Party of Northern Ireland. Many of those who become involved do so in the first instance due to experiences of paramilitary intimidation or 'punishment beatings'. This once again illustrates the importance of the reasons for formation, and the organizational evolution of a group for the question of participation.

While groups like FAIT try to attract as broad a coalition of support as possible, other P/CROs, such as Women Together, impose structural limitations on participation. The essential criteria for participation within Women Together are gender related. Everyone involved in the organization from the outset was a woman and this remains a condition of participation. There is no feminist ideological dimension to this. It is a practical goal to target women in the conflict and provide an opportunity for them to give voice to their fears and concerns in an environment that provides the space for them to do so. It was felt that the absence of the dominating presence of men was the only way to encourage women to open up, speak for themselves and voice their fears about the political situation. Many of those who became involved in Women Together in its early days in the 1970s, would have been Christians rather than atheists. This, of course, reflected the balance in society as a whole. However, this was not an overt ideological principle within the organization.

Regardless of the social profiles of their activists, it would be fair to say that the general public perception of Women Together is that it is a middle-class, middle-aged organization, populated by, at best, well-meaning do-gooders, at worst, by politically motivated cranks. A representative of the group believed that this 'happy clappy' image was a myth, and that the social profile of participants was diverse and

[4] The word 'moderate' is used here to indicate the Alliance Party's position between the nationalist and unionist blocs. It would be fair to say that the party occupies a space between the SDLP and the UUP, though it may best be described as a liberal unionist party. This does not ignore the view that some people would reject the notion that the Alliance Party of Northern Ireland occupies a 'moderate' political position.

balanced. 'I would say it is definitely not a middle-class organization, because we have members from all backgrounds and living in all areas. I mean, if I try to think of one middle-class woman that is very actively involved at the moment, I would have difficulty.'[5] When a member of Women Together was questioned about the overt political affiliations of people involved in the group, she suggested that there was no specific political identification within the staff or membership, though she went on to comment: 'I suppose we would have quite a few Alliance [Party] voters and members of the Alliance Party amongst our membership.'[6] While the party-political identification of Women Together is diverse (they also have Ulster Unionist and SDLP members), there is certainly a preponderance of participants with liberal attitudes towards conflict resolution and social change. The overriding attitude amongst those involved in the organization is one of 'live and let live' and this is translated into the political outlook of the organization and the activities it engages in. There is a significant degree of overlap between the group and similar P/CROs and activists often have dual membership of Women Together and other complementary groups. 'We have members who have been involved with Corrymeela since the early days of Corrymeela, with Protestant and Catholic Encounter (PACE), with integrated education [organizations] from the very early days.'[7]

While they differ fundamentally from the ideological focus evident within single-identity groups such as UCAN (Londonderry), the ethos is remarkably similar for both organizations. A sense of moral duty to serve a beleaguered community underpins the thinking and activity of both groups, although Women Together defines that community in the wider context of Northern Ireland as a whole, rather than working-class Protestants in the Waterside area of Derry. Both are driven by a desire to make a positive contribution to their defined communities, and infused with sufficient enthusiasm and optimism to believe that they can make a difference.

The activists within human rights organizations in Northern Ireland, such as FAIT and the Committee on the Administration of Justice (CAJ), could be said to be rather harder-edged than those

5 Representative of Women Together. Interview with authors, 13 March 1997.
6 Ibid.
7 Ibid.

participating in reconciliation organizations such as Women Together. The sense of moral indignation often evident in the latter generic grouping, is more frequently expressed in terms of a sense of 'injustice' by the former. The typical CAJ activist is middle-class, well-educated (often with a legal background), and committed to the concept of civil liberties. While the organization attracts a cross section of people from the unionist and nationalist communities, there are also a large number of people who would not classify their political attitudes along these traditional lines. The political bias is less towards nationalism or unionism than towards liberalism and a commitment to contributing to progressive social change within Northern Ireland.

One of the most interesting P/CROs working within Northern Ireland in recent years was the Peace Train organization. It was formally two organizations, with management committees in Northern Ireland and the Irish Republic. The original Northern Committee was composed of prominent political and cultural figures such as Paddy Devlin, trade-unionist and former member of the SDLP, and Belfast-based writer Sam McAughtry, amongst others. The Peace Train was unusual for a number of reasons. It was one of the few P/CROs that was constituted on a bi-national basis. With respect to the issue of participation, the Peace Train was also unorthodox in being proactive in the manner in which it selected its activists. It is clear that the Northern Committee was not formed in a haphazard manner by the first people to declare an interest in the organization, but was selected along an existing social network for reasons of religious and political balance, and public recognition of the personnel. This served to create a predominantly male, 40+ profile for the organization, as those using their social networks mostly fell into that category. One former activist within the Peace Train pointed out that staffing peace organizations is often difficult because individuals who seek to fill these sorts of roles are often active within several other areas or organizations: 'There is a danger in making appointments in peace groups, where people are highly motivated but perhaps are wearing more than one hat.'[8]

For some organizations, such as the Springfield Inter-Community

8 Representative of the Peace Train. Interview with authors, 17 June 1997.

Development Project (SICDP), the nature of the social and political profile of their activists is of central importance to their activities. To other groups such as the Peace Train, FAIT, or the Ulster People's College, this is a peripheral matter. Because of its role as an inter-community project, dealing with unionists and nationalists within interface areas of Belfast, the Project needs to reflect the communities it works within. All of those involved in the SICDP, both at a staff and management level, have substantial experience of community work, and the vast majority of those involved are from a working-class background. In political terms, the participants are mixed in terms of the 'sectarian divide' in Northern Ireland, containing people with both loyalist and republican political affiliations. The project manager, Billy Hutchinson, is a leading figure within the Progressive Unionist Party, while another member of staff comes from the republican community. A previous member of the management committee was Pat McGeown, who took part in the republican hunger strike in 1981 and was a key figure in Sinn Féin until his death in 1997. Another member of Sinn Féin has taken McGeown's place on the management committee, working alongside another member of the PUP.

The SICDP have made a conscious effort to ensure that eight of the management committee's sixteen members represent the republican/nationalist community while the other eight represent the loyalist/unionist community. It would be fair to say that there are not many participants within the Project who would be identified with middle-class 'moderate' political groupings such as the Alliance Party. The reason for this unusual spread of political opinions within the management committee is entirely functional and pragmatic, as their representation provides access for the Project into those communities, and provides the initial credibility to enable the organization to get involved with such groups. In contrast to the pattern evident within the Peace Train, these individuals were appointed to the management committee, not because of their own personal profiles within society or other organizations, but because they were working within the community and would bring practical skills and benefits to the Springfield Project. It was pointed out that the pattern of participation within management structures was not an arbitrary issue, but was of fundamental importance to the viability of the organization:

> It was imperative at the start that I had credibility on this side [of the interface]. Being an ex-prisoner and being in [prison] a long time [was important]. Had someone come in from outside, unknown, this project wouldn't have got off the ground. They would have been viewed with great scepticism and suspicion by people. People on this side [nationalist/republican] view community relations as some sort of British counter-insurgency movement you know. So we had to have a street credibility.[9]

Another interesting feature of those involved in the Springfield Project, is that many of them, even those who differ fundamentally in their political orientations, have known one another for many years and share a mutual respect. This has been an important factor in helping to establish trust within the group and engender a viable working relationship within the organization. As Northern Ireland is a relatively small place, those involved in community development work inevitably meet one another on a regular basis attending the same conferences in pursuit of the same grants, and cannot avoid getting to know one other. This has helped to foster a trust and confidence between many of the individuals concerned within the sector.

Finding recruits and keeping them

Once a P/CRO becomes established, gets a level of funding and plans a range of activities, a key concern facing many groups is how to find activists to carry out the work and how to provide incentives to hold on to them. Strategies for doing this vary depending on the nature of the organization. Small groups such as UCAN (Londonderry) with cohesive communities and limited catchment areas will often use informal grapevines to attract recruits. 'They hear about us. You just know people and they come up to you and say, "Look, can I help you?"'[10] This mechanism of recruitment is possible because UCAN operates in a small tightly-knit community where everybody knows one another. Such a strategy would not be as effective for larger, more formalized groups.

9 Representative of the Springfield Inter-Community Development Project. Interview with authors, 6 October 1997.

10 Representative of UCAN (Londonderry). Interview with authors, 10 March 1997.

There is certainly little obvious material incentive for people to become involved in small P/CROs like UCAN. A member of the organization suggested that the only benefit participants derived was a sense of achievement at 'seeing the job done' and the fulfilment of having made a positive contribution to their community: 'They want to make a difference, I mean if we don't make a difference, who is going to do it?'[11] A familiar claim was that it was more like a cause than a job. When a representative of UCAN was asked why people left the organization, the familiar themes of economic deprivation and ethnic embattlement were put forward. Certainly a big factor for small community development groups in the loss of personnel relates to the economics of the region. There are very few jobs in the Derry area, especially in the city, which people can apply for, or perhaps feel safe applying for. Consequently, most of the jobs that do become available, draw people away from the locality and thus lessen their involvement with the group.

> The jobs in Protestant areas are very hard to come by. Very few will actually go across the town to get a job. I mean [of] all the 300 Seagate jobs that John Hume brought [to Derry], no Protestants applied for them. Fair employment [legislation] isn't working properly for Protestants. You take all the major companies in this town, Seagate, Fruit of the Loom, all the American companies . . . every one of them – Derry City Council – has a very bad ratio for jobs for Protestants. It is unbelievable, the job deficiencies in the work force for Protestants.[12]

Regardless of its accuracy, it is clear from this statement that the alienation of such single-identity P/CROs extended to the internal structures of the organization. While there is no doubting the sincerity of the feelings, it would be fair to say that there is a tendency within both sides of the community in Northern Ireland to blame their difficulties on others and to adopt a fatalistic perspective that tends to reduce the responsibilities of the identity group.

Many other small P/CROs such as FAIT, share UCAN's informal and ad hoc methods for attracting activists. There are no preferred types of participant, save that they would accept and support the central ethos of the organization and would be opposed to paramilitary

[11] Ibid.
[12] Ibid.

punishment beatings and intimidation. FAIT's recruitment strategy is quite basic, with staff and members of the executive committee spreading the word through their own contacts within the community and in networking within other similar organizations. As new volunteers come in younger blood is introduced and their network of contacts will be used where possible. More formalized approaches, such as placing advertisements in the newspapers requesting support, or asking people directly to join, have not been used, partly due to lack of funding but also because FAIT does not see itself essentially as a membership-based organization, but as working in a more immediate way with people who are under direct threat from the paramilitaries. The benefits of participation are provided by a sense of being able to make some contribution to the social fabric of Northern Ireland. Those involved with FAIT are motivated by a feeling that they are helping to reduce the human rights abuses taking place within society. One of the leading figures in the organization provided the following explanation for participation:

> I think people that get involved with FAIT must like having abuse heaped on them! Perhaps it keeps the adrenaline flowing? They are people who are genuinely concerned about what is happening in Northern Ireland, and they want to make some kind of a contribution to try and stop that. I think anybody who gets involved in an organization like FAIT has got a lot of courage to begin with, and a lot of commitment. [It is not financial] . . . For instance, all the Executive Committee members over the last twelve or eighteen months, no matter where they are travelling to, no matter where they're going, if it is within a one-hundred-mile radius they get no expenses. They get no contributions at all towards their phone bills. That all comes out of our own pockets.[13]

FAIT is a P/CRO that adopts a confrontational approach to paramilitary organizations. Consequently, participation in the organization is often quite high profile and requires a degree of commitment, especially given the poor level of funding available to the group. Dealing with the victims of punishment attacks and lobbying on their behalf is a stressful and time-consuming activity and often leads to burn-out in participants.

Other P/CROs are more driven by the activities of their members than by the activities of the committee or the staff. Women Together

[13] Representative of FAIT. Interview with authors, 14 March 1997.

recruits more actively than FAIT and uses its membership in a more proactive way. Its primary method of recruitment is by word of mouth. One person joins, they tell their friends what the organization is about and the word gets spread on a range of different personal and social networks. Women Together also goes out into the community to recruit positively, using public events to bring people into the organization.

> I was out at the Women's Festival [in Co. Antrim] and we put up display stands and go out and talk to people. We would send speakers along to the local groups. We would do articles for the local press. We are looking at organizing a letter campaign with children in the county Antrim area at the moment, just to raise the profile. It's all about raising the profile. We also have people who just phone and say, 'Look, I've heard of you, I want to join'. We have information packs, which we send out to them encouraging them to become involved, and then we bring them in to a new members' session to learn more about the organization.[14]

Some members of Women Together have been active within the group since its inception and remain heavily involved, while others are essentially 'paper' members. The organization rarely sees them from one year to the next unless there is a very special event or crisis. Many of these people are committed to helping the organization but have too many other responsibilities to devote time to active participation. Such people may become actively involved if changes to their personal circumstances leave them with more free time, or following a particular event such as a bombing or a riot within their area. The Drumcree stand-off in July 1996 was one example when paper members got on the phone to ask what the organization was doing and how they could help. However, as the following comment suggests, the heightening of sectarian tensions can be a double-edged sword for P/CROs in Northern Ireland. On one level, such an incident can emphasize the relevance of, and necessity for, peace/conflict resolution work and refocus the commitment of activists who may have drifted away from the organization due to apathy or changing personal circumstances. On the other hand, an increase in sectarian violence may have the opposite effect, causing disillusionment among activists and a fatalistic resignation that their best efforts have not been able to prevent community conflict.

[14] Representative of Women Together. Interview with authors, 13 March 1997.

> The marching issue has really got people going. And then it can work the other way as well, because when there is more fear in the community and feelings of helplessness and hopelessness, we've had some members who have said, 'Look, I've been involved for ten years, I've done my best, nothing's changing, what's the point'.[15]

As in the case of FAIT, the primary reason for activists leaving Women Together was burn-out, both physical and emotional: 'It's a lot to do with people getting tired, specially with members who have been involved for a long time, some of whom at this moment in time are feeling that sort of burn-out.'[16] People also leave the organization for more practical reasons, such as getting a new job, which may take them out of their local community. The changing role of women in society and the increased employment opportunities has also, ironically, had a negative impact upon membership.

> If you go back twenty-six years to when Women Together formed, many women were not working. An awful lot of women were at home with their children. There weren't a lot of social activities, there weren't the leisure centres. . . . But look what there is now for women. And also you have a lot of responsibilities with children and everything. So you maybe are very keen, especially if you are motivated by something Women Together have done, or something that's happened in society, and you desperately want to become involved, but you find that when you join, you just haven't an awful lot of time.[17]

There is a sense of moral missionary zeal about some P/CROs such as Women Together which, in more specifically focused human rights organizations, such as the Committee on the Administration of Justice (CAJ), gets expressed through language such as 'justice' and 'rights'. It would also be fair to say that, unlike FAIT, the CAJ is a human rights group that points in the other direction, not at paramilitary activity, but at the state, its agencies and its legal apparatus. Consequently, it attracts people who are dissatisfied with the state's legislative and operational response to the political conflict. Of course, this does not mean that such people are not opposed to other sources of violence or injustice, simply that they operate on the principle that 'two wrongs do not make a right'. The CAJ operates on the

[15] Ibid.
[16] Ibid.
[17] Ibid.

premise that paramilitary violence will not be effectively addressed until the state puts in place a fair and just criminal justice system. There is also a practical point here, in that the lawyers who get involved with the CAJ have some leverage with the British government and can test its activities against European human rights norms. As the government claims to operate a just and democratic criminal justice system, human rights abuses can be highlighted as being inconsistent with such claims. Paramilitary groups, of course, make no such claims and cannot be held up to legal scrutiny or international embarrassment.

It was suggested by one member of the organization that those who were attracted to joining the CAJ and similar P/CROs were political with a small 'p', and were exasperated with the stalemate that had existed for the previous thirty years. Such people, it was argued, found the formal political system too sectarian to become involved in, and diverted their energies into the NGO sector, which had a much more practical and immediate impact on the issues that concerned them. In the case of the CAJ, this revolved around human rights abuses.

A representative from the CAJ was asked if there was a cultural difference between the group and other more reconciliation-focused P/CROs, or an organizational ethos that attracted people to the CAJ instead of overt 'peace' groups, such as the Corrymeela community or the Peace People? Were people attracted to the CAJ because they viewed its focus and remit as applied, 'cutting edge' conflict resolution work, rather than what they might regard as being the remote and unfocused reconciliation activity of other organizations? It was claimed in response, that the CAJ did tend to recruit those who wanted to channel their energies into the practical side of conflict resolution in an immediate 'firefighting' mode.

> [The CAJ] generally doesn't attract a kind of 'happy-clappy', 'let's bring our beanbags and spread the pollen of peace' type person, you know? Part of that is legal, legal in the sense that people who are involved in the legal system or whatever, maybe don't tend to be of that disposition, they tend to be a bit more kind of hard-edged about human rights in particular you know? I suppose, speaking personally, I would never have been attracted to any of those kinds of organizations. I can see certainly that they do some good and valuable work, but it wouldn't be my ballpark.[18]

[18] Representative of the CAJ. Interview with authors, 2 June 1997.

Activists with a legal background and an interest in human rights issues are sometimes attracted to this P/CRO because there are things that it is possible to do within the CAJ context that a lawyer would be restricted from doing in private practice, where the first concern is with the client rather than the rights or wrongs of a particular civil liberties issue. While casework is also involved, there is a significant policy-oriented and campaigning role in the CAJ, which is a radical departure from the more orthodox legal role. In common with the other P/CROs studied, the motivation for those who work within the CAJ comes from a sense of 'making a difference', both in terms of individual miscarriages of justice and on the wider human rights policy agenda. Many of those active within the CAJ at either managerial or staff level, believe that the organization has clout and is listened to and has had a real and appreciable impact at the policy-making level. 'You really do feel [connected to the policy process] . . . and unlike most people you actually have an opportunity to input into the debate that's going on around what direction you should go in as a society, so I think that's the most gratifying thing.'[19]

The CAJ has a very public profile in Northern Ireland and those who become involved with it are normally very committed people, aware of what the group does and what it stands for. Consequently, short-term disillusionment is rare and has tended to occur within a much longer time frame, with some of those who became involved in the early days of the CAJ, when it was primarily an academic legal think tank, being less comfortable about the organization's move across into direct activism and individual casework.

> From the late 1980s onwards you had an increased professionalism in the CAJ in two directions. Firstly, in terms of international mobilization we connected well with other human rights organizations. We started to use international instruments; we started to use the UN and use Geneva and all those places much more successfully, and so we moved in a kind of international-plane direction. Parallel with that, thankfully, we also had staff in particular, who were very good at community work. So, parallel with getting quite 'hot-shottish' around international stuff, we also developed very good links into the communities. We developed very good links with victims of human rights abuses. [We] connected into a lot of those, into the families of those miscarriages of justice cases. [We] connected very well [and] worked quite hard at connecting into loyalist groups in particular. . . . We got much better at what we did

[19] Ibid.

> basically. There are probably people around who quite liked the old [ways], you know? . . . There were probably people who would have been much happier for us to be diddling along and saying nice and worthy things, but actually not making a huge amount of difference. So those kind of people probably did drift. We were not shirking controversial issues; we would have been seen to be not shirking controversial issues. There were probably people who were uncomfortable with that.[20]

It is clear that the key to participation within P/CROs in Northern Ireland is the sense of 'making a difference'. It is the practical impact and the belief that they are making a positive contribution to society that motivates the majority of people to become involved in this sector. The Ulster People's College provides a very similar picture. It seems that people were attracted to the ideal of the group and what it stood for as a community-based educational facility. More specifically, participants were attracted by the organizational ethos, which focused on overcoming social disadvantage through education and training. There was also a feeling (like the CAJ attitude to the orthodox political process) that the formal educational institutions were not catering to a section of the population and that the College had an approach to learning that combined education with action in a way that was not possible within the normal classroom setting. It was argued that this organizational ethos was embodied within the College's Community Development programme, which was aimed at community groups rather than simply individuals within them.

> We are an organization that actually is targeting community organizations for their participation on the programme. We don't just simply send application forms out to them, hoping that they will reply to us, we actually target community organizations on the ground, and we target them over a period of three to five years, so that we have a continuity of people from a project. So you are not simply developing the skills of the individual, but of the project or the group itself, which then makes a far greater contribution to the actual community from which they come. Our other interest in the programme is not simply the individual, it's the whole class as a group, who then become a network, both during the year that they are with us, but we then try to keep that networking process going by bringing students here periodically to have a look at policy changes. . . . So we are not simply bringing them here for a year and letting them go after they have got their accreditations from the

[20] Ibid.

> university. We actually see ourselves as being part and parcel of the developmental process of the individual and the organization. I think that's the difference between working here and working somewhere else.[21]

Community development groups, such as the Clogher Valley Rural Development Centre, fit neatly into a pattern of communitarianism evident within the more explicit peace and human rights organizations discussed above. It is clear that the incentive for involvement comes from a feeling of success, of contributing to the area, of making a practical difference to the resources and amenities of the local community. Beyond that there is also a desire among the activists to decrease sectarianism and increase cross-community contact within the region. The Clogher Centre focuses on the twin goals of localized community development on the one hand and cross-community relations on the other. A representative from the organization was asked how these goals related to the interests and incentives for involvement of the participants. Was there any difference within the management team, for example, between people who became involved primarily to improve community relations and those whose main goal was to provide resources for their area?

> The Management Committee would be very much aware of the fact that it is obviously a neutral venue. . . . They would be very much aware that cross-community and neutrality is the key thing in all this. I mean it has to be that way. . . . So, if they want to become involved in this group then they have to accept that as the ethos of it. It's not to come in here to make sure that the Protestant community is getting their bit or to make sure that the Catholic community is [getting theirs]. It's more to try [to develop] . . . a progressive way of what can be done for the people of the Valley, irrespective of religion because . . . in that aspect, religion doesn't come into it. . . . We're thinking here of 200 farm families in the Clogher Valley, we're not thinking [of] 100 Catholic [and] 100 Protestant [families].[22]

One of the most interesting P/CRO groups in Northern Ireland with regard to the nature of its participants, was the Peace Train organiza-

21 Representative of the Ulster People's College. Interview with authors, 10 September 1997.

22 Representative of the Clogher Valley Rural Development Centre. Interview with authors, 16 June 1997.

tion. While most of the activists were united in being inconvenienced by the blowing-up of the Belfast–Dublin railway line, and were opposed in a general sense to politically motivated violence, the participants had little else in common. Most of those who became active in the Peace Train were attracted by the idea that they could do something practical and positive to indicate their opposition, rather than simply sitting back passively and accepting that they could do nothing about paramilitary violence. It has been suggested that people became involved in the organization because it was activity based, in contrast to the rather preachy, worthy groups of the 1970s such as the Peace People.

However, the question of why people left the Peace Train is perhaps more interesting than the issue of why they joined it, and tells us more about the nature of those who participated in it. A former leading representative from the organization was asked if people left due to a sense of burn-out, or due to feelings of frustration and failure at the fact that their activity had not stopped the bombings. Alternatively, did people leave because of personality clashes or ideological disputes following arguments over what the Peace Train was doing or what it was not doing?

> I think [people left for] a combination of reasons. I would have said very little of it would have been burn-out. Some of it would have been questioning should the Peace Train be going on? Where does this end up? Do we become just another peace organization, ineffectual, and if so, is there something else I can give time and energy to that will give a greater sense of satisfaction? I think . . . when you hear people saying that they're into ideological fallouts, I always think they're constructing a nice comfortable position for something a bit more pragmatic. I mean I certainly was not aware that there was anything of such difference that [it] could never have been resolved and accommodated if people had wanted to work at it, and if people didn't want to work at it, I suspect it was because they felt that there were other issues, or other organizations, that they could get involved in or give their time to, and not the Peace Train.[23]

It is clear that the reasons why people left the Peace Train were influenced by their initial motivations for joining it. As many had always regarded it as a transient single-issue group, leaving was for some, as natural an act as joining. For those who perceived it as being a more permanent fixture with an evolving remit from the specific focus of

[23] Representative of the Peace Train. Interview with authors, 15 August 1997.

the bombing of the railway line, to the more general issue of politically motivated violence, the exit from the group was more acrimonious. There were fundamental disagreements within the organization about its focus and activities, together with simple personality clashes and petty jealousy over manoeuvring for power. This was not helped by the fact that the Peace Train was made up of two autonomous groups with their own agendas. Eventually, frictions within the Southern Committee (that got to the stage where one aggrieved party threatened to take legal action against the organization) infected the relationships within the Northern Committee and led directly to at least one resignation from an office-bearing position.

Apart from the split along the lines of personality, there was also a fault line between those who saw the Peace Train as a very focused single-issue group and those who believed it should broaden its remit into other areas of peace campaigning. In a private memo to the committee members of the Peace Train, the aggrieved parties from the Southern Committee alleged that an individual had been prevented from resuming her office as Dublin Secretary after a short absence due to illness, and accused another member of the Southern Committee of leaking confidential minutes to *Phoenix* magazine, which had subsequently published a series of embarrassing stories about the Peace Train. Ironically perhaps, this was a P/CRO that seemed to have more difficulty managing conflict within the organization than in dealing with opposition from the paramilitary groups it was established to confront.

While some P/CROs in Northern Ireland take a rather ad hoc 'first come first served' approach to recruiting activists, the Springfield Inter-Community Development Project is rather more precise in this regard. This is due to structural reasons relating to the fact that it is primarily a community development group rather than a reconciliation or human rights-based organization. Its inter-community focus demands that participation and representation at staff and management levels is balanced between the nationalist and unionist communities.

As with most P/CROs studied, the Springfield Project recruits staff through a formal selection procedure that conforms to the fair employment legislation in Northern Ireland. Posts are advertised in local newspapers and candidates are appointed on the basis of merit.

While Fair Employment Commission rules only apply to organizations that employ over ten people, it was important for the organization to be *seen* to recruit fairly, in order to retain its credibility within republican and loyalist areas. There is an organizational necessity for the Project to employ staff from both sides of the community. Because the staff team is very small (five when studied in 1997) it can sometimes be difficult to ensure equal representation within a policy which simply recruits on the individual merits of the applicant.

As with the Clogher Valley Rural Development Centre, the central motivation for involvement in the Springfield Project comes from a desire to engage in community development, to participate in improving the social and economic conditions of the local community, and to make some sort of difference or contribution at this local level. The picture of what motivates individuals is complicated in that, for many people, the initial involvement comes at some level of self-interest (i.e. how can the work of the Project benefit them or the rest of their community in a practical way), rather that out of some sense of theoretical altruism or communitarian spirit. Also, first contact/knowledge is often with the work that the Springfield Project has initiated, rather than with the organization itself.

Clearly then, motivations for eventual participation in the structure of inter-community P/CROs such as the Springfield Project are varied and complex, though the basic motivation would come from some sense of community commitment. The core reason for activism would be to assist those within working-class areas who have been marginalized socially and economically, to make them aware of their rights and entitlements, and to help them secure these rights and improve their situations. Another motivation to participation relates to the political opinions of many of those most heavily involved, in that they see the community development approach as providing the only secure foundations for any chance of progressive change to take place within Northern Ireland. Many are committed ideologically to a community development strategy as an agent of progressive social change within their society. In this sense, people believe in the *theoretical* model as much as they do in the *actual specifics* of the work that takes place, though obviously the one reinforces the other. The lead normally comes from the community rather than from the Project. The Project will try to find out what the needs of the community group are (or what that group thinks they are) and will try to provide what help it can. The hope is that as trust and confidence develops within the community, it will begin to see that the Project can help to tackle issues such as drug abuse, poverty, housing problems and sectarianism. Part of the battle for P/CROs like the Springfield Project is building up the confidence of the communities to look beyond their own areas, into 'the other' community. This was thought to be a particularly acute problem within the Protestant working-class population: 'It is not just a fear; it is also not recognizing that they have a contribution to make, and that their contribution can shape their future. I think that in many cases we point that out to people.'[24]

It is clear from the evidence available that a common theme exists within the NGO sector with respect to the type of people who become involved in P/CROs, and that their motivations for doing so are remarkably similar. This could be characterized as those people 'with a bit of get up and go', often high-energy individuals with a degree of optimism that their involvement can make a positive contribution to their community, however they define that. Such people are frequently motivated to join a P/CRO out of frustration or moral indignation at the symptoms of the political conflict, such as economic deprivation, paramilitary violence, educational underachievement, or human rights abuses.

Expectations of P/CRO activists

The expectations of participants within P/CROs vary depending on the size of the organization and the level of its professionalization. In larger, established groups with a significant number of salaried staff, there is often a formal employer/employee relationship with line-management structures and disciplinary procedures. The smaller organizations, which survive on voluntary effort, are typically more ad hoc. However, a general NGO ethos pervades most of the P/CROs in Northern Ireland, where a culture of trust is promoted, with participants being given responsibilities and expected to fulfil them using their own initiative and resources.

24 Representative of the Springfield Inter-Community Development Project. Interview with authors, 5 September 1997.

UCAN (Londonderry) is a good example of a small P/CRO that imposes few expectations on its activists. When a member of the management committee was asked what demands were placed on participants, the answer was that 'there are no demands on your time. If you can do it, you do it, it's as simple as that; and if you can't, you can't. You're here because you want to be here. There are no set hours'.[25] It was claimed that there was no official line management or hierarchical chain through job descriptions or contracts, which a larger organization with paid employees would have. This 'easy come, easy go' informality within the group was regarded as an asset, making the people involved highly motivated and providing the type of flexibility that would not be available in larger organizations. It was suggested that one of the attractions of UCAN was the possibility that someone could come straight in off the street and receive immediate assistance, without bureaucratic complications.

A similar degree of flexibility was evident within Quaker House, a P/CRO that has little else in common with UCAN other than its small size. The remit for Quaker House is left open to the two members of staff to decide, in consultation with their support group and committee. It is certainly not a job in the conventional sense with set hours, or terms and conditions that require an expected commitment. 'I think nobody would criticize us if we put on the answer phone at five o'clock. But when you're here you're on duty really. Someone rang us at 1.47 a.m. a few nights ago when we were fast asleep and said, "How do I become a Quaker?" So it isn't a nine-to-five job.'[26]

While most of the P/CROs studied were populated by highly motivated volunteers and employees, and groups could tolerate varying levels of commitment depending upon the role of the participant and nature of the organization, less flexibility was shown on questions concerning ethical behaviour. Dishonesty, especially relating to the misappropriation of funds, is a disciplinary offence in every organization examined, and in one P/CRO led to the effective dismissal of an employee. While this issue is relatively clear-cut since

[25] Representative from UCAN (Londonderry). Interview with authors, 10 March 1997.

[26] Representative from Quaker House. Interview with authors, 26 March 1997.

groups would be forced to discipline such activists or risk having their funding withdrawn, law-breaking that conflicted with the ethos of the organization was a more complex area, especially if such behaviour was politically motivated or related in some way to the focus or activities of the group. In an effort to test the limits of acceptability within P/CRO organizations in Northern Ireland, the staff of Quaker House were asked what would happen in the hypothetical situation that a member of their support group was arrested and charged with a crime. If they joined the Protestant picket of Catholic churchgoers at Harryville[27] and got arrested for creating a breach of the peace, would they be disciplined and expelled from the organization? Their response illustrates the degree of tolerance exhibited by many P/CROs in Northern Ireland and an optimistic belief that dialogue and engagement with the particular individual could resolve the situation:

> I think if [that did happen] we would feel urgently that we wanted to talk it through as a group . . . and I could see possibly that an outcome of that might mean that the group might feel that Quaker House should be a bit more proactive in making contact with the loyalist protesters. I mean, it is a very unlikely situation, but I can see that if there was some concern, or such strong concern from one person, that they needed to go and stand there, then the outcome of that might be that the whole group might recognize that there was some sort of lack of communication with the protesters' side, that might mean that we should do something more active. Not support them [the Harryville protesters] in that way but possibly ask if we could talk with them. It wouldn't be any more than that, but that might be enough for the person to feel in tune with the group, and if it didn't, if they felt it was not enough, then I think we would say, 'Well, you know, if we feel quite clearly as a group that we can't go along with such a strong expression or view, do you really think [that] you are in tune with this?' And the person would have to answer that question and they might feel they wanted to resign. But I think it would be that way round, rather than the group saying, 'You're not wanted any more'. I don't think it would ever happen like that; the onus would be put much more on the person to make it clear whether they were in tune with the group.[28]

The Ulster People's College is a good example of a larger professionalized P/CRO that has normal employer/employee expectations and

[27] This picket was a symptom of the general parades dispute and was an issue in 1997 when the interview took place.

[28] Representative from Quaker House. Interview with authors, 5 September 1997.

hierarchical line-management structures. However, as with many other groups in Northern Ireland, a great deal of care is taken to ensure that participants are given autonomy and responsibility to do their work, and the internal culture is based on trust within the organization. Of course, the College regards itself as being more than simply another educational facility, having a clear sense of purpose and a clear set of strategic objectives to combine the provision of education with progressive social change. Participation, therefore, in the Ulster People's College and many other P/CROs within Northern Ireland, requires a level of commitment from the individual to the aims of the group. A representative from the College was asked whether employees were expected to buy into a particular organizational ethos. Did they need to demonstrate, for example, a commitment to the idea of progressive social change? To test the limits of expectation, two hypothetical examples were suggested. Firstly, what would happen if somebody, in their own personal capacity, who happened to be a loyalist and happened to be paid to work at the College, took part in the Harryville picket and got arrested for blocking a road in a non-violent political protest? Would such behaviour be deemed to be embarrassing to the College or against its organizational ethos and therefore a disciplinary offence? Secondly, what would happen if somebody got arrested for possession of an illegal drug that was clearly for their own personal 'recreational' use as opposed to a dealing offence? The initial reaction to these (admittedly lurid) scenarios, was to claim that the College would not get into such a position because of the recruitment techniques it used. The more detailed prescription that followed, however, was remarkably similar to that of Quaker House, in refusing to denigrate the individual and seeking to understand and address the motivation behind such behaviour.

> We have unionists and nationalists in the staff team and we have people who go on protests. They're more likely to go on a trade union protest, in terms of the cuts, or in terms of wanting to actually get all-inclusive talks or whatever. So it depends. It's not an issue about whether somebody's caught doing something in an individual way, whether it's smoking pot – I mean for me that's not a major issue . . . it's a question of whether it is respectful or disrespectful, or how that would be perceived. Now if somebody's caught 'peggin' bricks', it's disrespectful to another community, you know? So it's actually what it stands for, and you would want to talk that through with the person and what made them [do it].

> What I'm saying is that there is an ethos here which attracts people, and we have strong unionists who work with us on our voluntary and on our wider tutor team as well as in our current tutor team, as well as nationalists, but they are still tested out in relation to an ethos which is actually about being people-oriented. . . . It's about how people respect and work with one another, which is actually the bottom line.[29]

When a representative from the Springfield Inter-Community Development Project was questioned about these ethical issues and what it would take to break or contravene the organizational ethos of the Project, the response indicated the importance of structure and focus within P/CROs. It contrasts with the position of the Ulster People's College in that the less overtly political example of a participant being arrested for 'smoking pot' was considered more dangerous to the credibility of the group than attendance at the Harryville picket. The interviewee explained that such attendance would not be seen as a disciplinary offence. It would not be condoned but would be viewed as the personal right of the individual to engage in such an activity. In common with the approach of other groups such as Quaker House and the Ulster People's College, it was pointed out that far from condemning such an action, the group would use it to open up a debate within the organization over the issue and to talk the matter through in terms of why the individual engaged in such behaviour and how they saw this in terms of their work within the Project: '[That sort of activity] wouldn't be seen as contradicting the ethos, because I think the group is about inclusiveness and it is about providing an opportunity for every shade of opinion to have its space and have its say.'[30]

Interestingly, questions about personal ethics were considered more problematic than those about political ethics. When offered the hypothetical situation that a member of the Project at staff or management committee level was arrested for a drugs offence, the interviewee stated that this would cause greater difficulties for the Project than more publicly controversial issues such as the Harryville example. It was pointed out that the Springfield Project was heavily involved with young people in the area and in social issues, one of

[29] Representative of the Ulster People's College. Interview with authors, 27 August 1997.

[30] Representative of the Springfield Inter-Community Development Project. Interview with authors, 13 August 1997.

which was the problem of substance abuse (drug-taking, glue-sniffing, problems associated with alcohol abuse). If someone in the organization was arrested for substance abuse, it would be highly embarrassing for the group and would reduce the credibility of the Project within the community: 'That would raise a considerable dilemma here, because we have been very outspoken on substance-abuse issues.'[31]

Conclusion

It is clear from the evidence provided in this chapter that the expectations of participants within the P/CRO sector vary depending on the size of the organization, with larger groups demanding more from salaried employees than would be expected from unpaid volunteers. In most cases there was an NGO liberality and informality about hierarchy and attendance, with an emphasis being placed upon the importance of individual initiative and personal motivation. However, all of the groups studied suggested that participants were required to support, and adhere to, the organizational ethos and the values that underpinned this ethos, and that the behaviour of activists would be tested against these concepts rather than in response to isolated external events. The first section of this chapter detailing the personality of the typical P/CRO participant illustrates why organizations are rarely required to conduct such tests. It is seldom a career path attractive to those interested in self-aggrandizement and is much more likely to appeal to those with a sincere interest in working for the benefit of their community, whether on a cross-community, inter-community, or single-identity basis. Of course, having a group of committed employees, volunteer activists and members is of little use to a P/CRO if it does not possess the resources to sustain its activities. It is ironic, therefore, that much of the effort of these organizations goes into raising and sustaining the funding to retain their activists and to pursue their programmes. As the next chapter will demonstrate, the constant struggle to secure funding is central to the P/CRO sector and in some cases can make or break the organization.

[31] Ibid.

6
Finding the Peace Pennies: Funding the P/CRO Sector in Northern Ireland

Introduction

At the beginning of the twenty-first century, funding is possibly the most important issue for the P/CRO sector as a whole. This chapter will address the following four themes, which emerged as the most significant during the course of our research:

1) How stable is funding within the P/CRO sector?
2) What strategies do these organizations use to maintain and develop new funding sources?
3) What ethical issues, if any, are involved for these groups in obtaining resources?
4) What is the nature of the relationship between P/CROs and their funders?

As with several other themes examined in this study, the range of issues with regard to finding and maintaining resources reflects the diversity of organizations that exist within Northern Ireland. The ten organizations of focus in the course of this research could be said to be representative of the P/CRO sector as a whole within Northern Ireland, to the extent that they incorporate small groups such as UCAN (Londonderry), which operates on an extremely small budget, through to larger P/CROs with annual incomes that run into six-figure sums. The following table provides a brief guide to the relative size of the ten organizations that form the backbone for the empirical data presented in this book. This table demonstrates that (aside from

TABLE 8: THE FUNDING LEAGUE TABLE[1]

	Ranked by Income from 1 to 10*	Annual Income over £50,000	Core-funded by one source
Ulster Community Action Network (UCAN) Londonderry	10	No	No
Peace Train	9	No	Yes
Women Together for Peace	8	No	Yes
Families Against Intimidation and Terror	7	No	Yes
Quaker House	6	No	Yes
Clogher Valley Rural Development Centre	5	No	No
Springfield Inter-Community Development Project	4	Yes	No
Committee on the Administration of Justice	3	Yes	No
Dove House Resource Centre	2	Yes	No
Ulster People's College	1	Yes	No

*with 10 being the lowest annual income and 1 being the highest.

[1] These figures relate to the period in 1997–98 when the research was carried out.

UCAN (Londonderry)), P/CROs that have diverse sources of funding are likely to be larger, while those that are reliant on one core funder, are likely to be smaller and have annual incomes under £50,000 a year. However, what the raw data does not tell us, and what is of most interest, is what sort of funding the P/CRO sector in Northern Ireland looks for. How does it attempt to get it? How successful is it at getting it? And what sort of problems does this present for the organizations concerned? The remainder of this chapter will seek to answer these questions.

Summary of the major funding issues

Obtaining funding is of little use to an organization unless it is able to maintain it and plan its activities on the assumption that it will have sufficient resources to carry them on. A number of patterns emerged from the research relating to the stability of P/CRO funding, the strategy P/CROs adopted to obtain funding, and the ethical questions that emerged. Firstly, the organizations studied could be separated into those groups that were able to operate on very limited resources, and those that required substantial external funding. It was clear that P/CROs in the first category were mainly campaigning pressure groups, while the latter category was dominated by community development organizations and P/CROs with a significant service delivery function.

Secondly, while groups that were relatively unsuccessful in obtaining funding were limited by resources as to what they were able to do, they had freedom to operate without any restrictions being imposed upon them by a 'third party', such as a funder. The larger P/CROs on the other hand, with relatively stable funding bases, possessed the resources to do more work than their poorer cousins, but ran a greater risk than smaller organizations of suffering 'mission drift' and following the priorities of the funding community, rather than pursuing the original focus of their organization. It is also clear that while large P/CROs might be viewed as being relatively successful in attracting funding, they are also susceptible to the danger of becoming dominated by the demands of their own organizational infrastructure and 'prisoners' of their own success, constantly searching for resources in an attempt to preserve existing jobs and maintain programmes and activities.

Thirdly, the funding structure of the P/CRO sector in Northern Ireland is generally stable, but short term in nature. Few organizations can rely on funding being provided in excess of a three-year grant cycle. Many groups are able to access specific project-related grants that may last for a period of six or twelve months, but they often have difficulty maintaining this work once the grant period expires. As such funding is 'ring-fenced' for project costs, it is of little benefit in terms of building up the infrastructure of the organization or allowing it to consolidate. Consequently, many P/CROs have the capacity to grow and take on new projects and activities, yet remain brittle, as these programmes can collapse when the money runs out.

The fourth issue regarding funding that this study raises is that the structure of the P/CRO, and its ideological focus, can have a direct bearing on the stability of its funding. For example, a campaigning group with an overtly political focus is not able to apply for charitable status and is thus excluded from accessing many private funding sources such as trusts and foundations. This legal restriction presents a danger that the ideological perspectives and activities of the P/CRO sector may be moulded and implicitly directed by the funding community in reformist rather than radical directions.

A fifth pattern to emerge from this study of P/CRO funding is that some groups have more ethical problems than others over who they receive resources from. While there are exceptions, it is clear that community development organizations have fewer problems here than human rights groups, who tend to deal with more divisive and sensitive issues between the two communities.

Finally, it is clear from the research carried out into the P/CRO sector in Northern Ireland that organizations engage in different fundraising strategies. The smaller groups tend to have a minimalist approach and reactive strategy, while the larger P/CROs engage in social networking with the funders and pursue a much more proactive and co-ordinated funding strategy. The latter approach tends to be the more effective in securing resources.

Stability of funding

For some P/CRO organizations in Northern Ireland funding is a relatively low priority. There are two main reasons for this. The first may be due to the cooperative nature of the venture and the cohesion of the community being served by the group. A second reason why funding might be a peripheral issue for a P/CRO may be if the group was funded by a parent organization on a secure and ongoing basis. UCAN (Londonderry) is an example of a group that falls into the first of these categories. It has no core funding from any source and no paid staff (at the time of study in 1997). The activity of UCAN (Londonderry) is made possible through local community assistance, e.g. the provision of furniture, paint and so on by friendly and sympathetic businesses. UCAN (Londonderry) has received money from the Northern Ireland Voluntary Trust to run conferences, though such money is normally ring-fenced and cannot be diverted into organizational running costs. Quaker House, while being a radically different type of organization from UCAN (Londonderry), was in a similar situation with regard to funding in that, although it had a budget that employed two core staff, this funding was extremely stable. Quaker House fell into the second category in being 100 per cent funded through its parent group, the Quaker Peace and Service Committee based in Britain. It did not (when the research was conducted in 1997) spend any time looking for money from funders other than this, and consequently had no worries about sources of funding or its stability. If the group needed more money it would apply to the Committee, and if it was considered to be a worthy cause, the money would be provided.

However, this financial stability is the exception rather than the rule, and most P/CROs in Northern Ireland spend significant amounts of time and organizational effort in trying to maintain and develop funding opportunities. It would be fair to say that the acquisition of resources holds a very high place on the P/CRO list of priorities, consumes vast amounts of organizational effort and diverts attention and energy away from the original ideological focus and *raison d'être* of the group. While few P/CROs are aware of it, or care to admit it, the acquisition of resources and the struggle to maintain the organizational infrastructure, once established, has a direct bearing on the type of people who participate, the decision-making patterns of the group and the focus of activities that are ultimately engaged in. Typically an evolution takes place, which can either alienate or force out many of the 'gifted amateurs' motivated to become involved by the initial focus of the organization, but with limited time to devote to it and little interest in developing formal organizational structures or financial strategies. Such people are often replaced over time by professional administrators, equally committed to the ideological ethos, but who place more emphasis on strategic development and have a greater ability to perpetuate and expand the resources of the organization. This may often lead to greater formality within relationships in the P/CRO, employer/employee hierarchies, line-management structures, greater centralization and accounting procedures. This evolutionary pattern can easily create tensions between the original activists and those who become involved in a later period. One of the founders of the Ulster People's College, for instance, expressed concern that the evolution of the organization and its growth, had altered its original character and the type of people who were involved in it, as 'gifted amateurs' were squeezed out by the professionals due to funding imperatives.

> We were very much pioneers. It was an exciting time because everybody was very enthused . . . there was a lot of enthusiasm, a lot of idealism, a feeling that here was something that could make an impact. So it was a very exciting period and a lot of people gave a lot of their time to the whole exercise. I gave a hell of a lot of my time to it. There wasn't a great deal of money around for community organizations, for non-governmental organizations. It was a matter of trying to survive, trying to find money, mainly from trusts and charities rather than government. The situation has changed totally today, although it has changed temporarily in that, although they are getting a lot of money it is maybe a bit of a fool's paradise, because it is likely to end in about a year or two's time [when the European funding as part of its contribution to the 'peace process' comes to an end]. Then they are all going to be faced with the same situation, and the problem about that is that if it means that the voluntary organizations have given too much to the professional workers and have stepped back [from the organization] themselves, then when those professional workers disappear, where are they? That is a big issue. It's just that the voluntary movement has always emphasized that it is a *voluntary* movement. It's people giving of their spare time, but there is a danger that it will become too professionalized. If it becomes too professionalized then there is a real issue there. What is the role of the volunteer then?[2]

Typically, many P/CROs are funded through a cocktail of different funding bodies which provide them with resources that vary in amount and time scale, from a three-month project-related grant to a

[2] Representative of the Ulster People's College. Interview with authors, 3 May 1997.

three-year contribution to core funding. The most striking aspect of the funding pattern within Northern Ireland to emerge from this research, is that nearly all of the groups surveyed obtained resources, either directly or indirectly, from the British government, which is arguably one of the protagonists within the conflict that the P/CROs are engaged in addressing. When the research was conducted in 1997–98, FAIT were 100 per cent funded by the British government, and had some security in the knowledge that it would have been difficult politically for the government to have cut this funding off from the only organization specifically campaigning against paramilitary intimidation and attacks. One of the leading activists within FAIT remarked, 'I would say that so long as the problem still exists, so long as there's bombings, so long as there's shootings, so long as there's mutilation beatings, then I couldn't really see a body like CCRU [Central Community Relations Unit] stopping our funding, because FAIT's necessary'.[3] Time would prove this to be a sanguine judgement. The main dilemma for FAIT was not the stability of its funding, so much as its low level. Due to the nature of the work done by the organization, and the political/ideological complexion of its activists, there was no real ethical problem for FAIT in accepting government money. People contacted the organization because they had just suffered or were being threatened with a paramilitary punishment attack. As a consequence, they typically had more immediate concerns than the source of FAIT's funding. Many of those outside the group (particularly within the republican community) were more critical of FAIT's source of funding and alleged that it was being used by the British government as an agent for propaganda.

One of the main problems for FAIT in establishing a stable funding base was that, due to the focus of its work and the rules that currently govern the NGO sector, it was not eligible to apply for charitable status because the nature of its activities was deemed to be political. Attempts to get money from private sources such as local businesses, were normally rebuffed with a standard letter wishing the group well, but claiming that the company budget had been allocated for the year. FAIT believed that the reason for this lack of support was that these businesses were frightened of being publicly aligned with FAIT

[3] Representative of FAIT. Interview with authors, 28 November 1996.

in case that resulted in paramilitary action against their premises or personnel: 'They will support us and they will praise us but they will not give us funding because perhaps they think that the paramilitaries "will hear about this" [and burn their businesses down].'[4] FAIT believed that two of the biggest funding obstacles they faced were the fact that they were not eligible to apply for charitable status (which automatically prevented them from applying for grants from private trusts and foundations), together with the fact that they were already core funded. While this allowed them to remain financially solvent, the level of funding was so low that it prevented them from engaging in the level of activity they thought was necessary, and from applying to other organizations for core funding since this would result in the loss of their existing funder.

Other P/CROs felt less secure about their funding than FAIT. Women Together, for instance, feels that it is constantly scrambling to maintain its resources. Women Together has to apply for core funding from the Community Relations Council (CRC) every three years, and like many groups, never receives guaranteed funding for longer than a three-year period. Their only preference in terms of funding sources relates to the length of the grant and that it is in the form of core funding over a period of years, rather than project-specific revenue which only lasts for a limited period, thus inhibiting developmental and planning work. A representative from Women Together was asked to explain the problems associated with short-term funding (e.g. one year) compared with long-term funding (e.g. three years) and the difficulties this presented for their organization:

> It's just the continuity factor. If we are talking about involving a member of staff or employing someone, as everybody knows, it can take up to a year to really induct someone into an organization and to get them fully integrated into the organization, working effectively and taking responsibility themselves. Also, when it came to ACE positions, [it was difficult] when we had a position for one year and that person had to leave and you had to bring in somebody new. It's the time and effort in training someone, and even in an admin post you are talking of a training programme of a month or six weeks, or up to two months before somebody is fully au fait with the post, and then, before you know it, it is coming to the end of the year. . . . It affects planning, and when you are such a small organization it takes time away for the co-ordinator . . .

4 Ibid.

> who could be doing other things which are so important within the organization.[5]

The essential problem, therefore, with short-term funding is its instability, leading to a lack of continuity, together with the fact that staff turnover is high due to the regulations (imposed by the ACE scheme) that make it difficult to keep staff in post for more than twelve months at a time. A representative from the Clogher Valley Rural Development Centre, for example, pointed out that the group's least stable source of funding related to ACE jobs. At the time the group was studied in 1997, there were eleven ACE workers at the Centre, a figure that had been reduced from fifteen due to government funding cutbacks in the ACE programme. 'If you talk about the Clogher Valley as a whole and not just the Centre, when I started here before the first ACE cuts there were fifty-five ACE posts throughout the Clogher Valley – they are now down to, I think, around about twenty-five to twenty-six.'[6]

The funding requirements of P/CROs in Northern Ireland can vary considerably, depending to a large extent on the type of NGO and the focus of its activities. Thus, community development groups such as the Clogher Valley Rural Development Centre, or the Springfield Inter-Community Development Project, which aim to deliver services on a regular basis to disadvantaged groups, are heavily reliant on having the staff and financial resources to carry this out. Single-issue campaigning organizations such as the Peace Train, on the other hand, required less in terms of the continuity of funding, as they were in a position to run activities periodically, whenever resources became available to them. When a former activist in the Peace Train was asked about the group's general level of funding, it was clear that the organization was able to function on an extremely low level of income for most of its existence, and was by nature, a rather frugal group.

> The first Peace Train [in 1989] was totally run on subscriptions lifted on the train and donations [amounting to] about £1,000. One cheque book with fifty cheques ran the organization for two years, from 22 November

5 Representative of Women Together for Peace. Interview with authors, 6 March 1997.

6 Representative of the Clogher Valley Rural Development Centre. Interview with authors, 16 June 1997.

> '89 to the 26 March '91. So it was pretty thrifty. . . . Then the Community Relations Council became involved and they provided funding of up to a maximum of £25,000 for a couple of years. Then if we wanted to do one-off events we just applied for [other] small grants. We always took up collections on the train and we always invited people to make subscriptions.[7]

One of the most interesting aspects of the Peace Train organization was that the Northern and Southern Committees had separate fundraising groups and behaved largely independently of one another. There is a certain irony in the fact that a P/CRO set up to campaign for the preservation of the infrastructural rail link between North and South was itself divided. While they acted in close co-operation with one another, and shared the financial cost of activities, each Committee had to sustain its own organizational base. As one former activist remarked: 'If we were doing a seminar here and could get funding for it, then we didn't expect any contribution from the South and vice versa; if they were doing something [in the Republic] there would be no contribution demanded from us.'[8] Funding issues differed between the two parts of the organization. The Southern Committee was not able to access public money in the way that their Northern partners could, and this led to a lower level of income and a concentration on looking for private donations. While the Southern Committee was less well resourced and operated almost exclusively on unpaid voluntary effort, it did not have an office base, unlike the Northern Committee, which was comparatively better financed but which operated with bigger overheads.

While the Peace Train may have been structurally complex, its funding was relatively straightforward. Other P/CROs in Northern Ireland that were more cohesive in organizational terms, operated within a much more complex funding environment. Some of these organizations that were relatively well resourced viewed their funding as being unstable in that while long-standing relationships may have existed with their main funders, the budget was composed from a cocktail of groups rather than coming from one central core funder. A senior figure in one of the larger P/CROs in our sample put it like this:

7 Representative of the Peace Train. Interview with authors, 15 August 1997.
8 Ibid.

> Most of our funders negotiate with [us] on a three-year basis and we've been funded by some of the same people for ten years and so in that sense it's been consistent. But I'd say it's unstable in that we don't have core support for what we do, we have to raise the money, and so I'd say it's fairly unstable in many respects and certainly any kind of expansion is fraught with difficulty. I mean it's not that we are constantly in a funding crisis but there is never any room for complacency, and when you add a new programme, [you have] to work out exactly how it's going to be funded, and the funding we secure for different elements of our work is at most for three years.[9]

It was clear from this perspective that the instability in funding for larger P/CROs did not create a fear that the group's existence was in jeopardy if a particular funder 'pulled the plug' on the organization, as is the case with some smaller groups who operate through a single funder. For larger organizations, funding instability is more a question of worrying about long-term trends in the funding base, and specifically, about decreases in funding rather than its removal. 'Yes, it's about diminishing funding and those organizations saying, "Look, you know, we've been funding this for a very long time," and normally foundations don't do that.'[10]

Fundraising strategies

Clearly the strategy employed by a P/CRO to obtain funding is a crucial factor in determining the group's success and the ability of the organization to develop its activities. Greater resources facilitate increased activity, which potentially leads to an enhanced public profile and a greater internal and external perception of organizational 'worth'.

The diversity of P/CROs within Northern Ireland has resulted in the development of a large range of funding strategies, from groups with rather minimalist techniques to those carefully tuned in to the funding culture of their existing and potential donor organizations. It would be accurate to say that the P/CROs with better developed social networks within the funding community are more successful at developing their funding strategies. These tend to be the larger

[9] Off-the-record comment by a representative of a major P/CRO in Belfast. Interview with authors, May 1997.

[10] Ibid.

organizations with staff specifically responsible for fundraising. The smaller groups have a typically more ad hoc approach and a more remote and formal relationship with the funding community. The larger organizations also tend to be more strategic in their funding strategy and more proactive. Thus, while the former might simply fill in application forms requesting funding, the latter will make informal approaches and have a greater understanding of the criteria and priorities of the prospective funders. It would be fair to say that the approach employed by the Springfield Inter-Community Development Project (while by no means the poorest P/CRO studied) was typical of many organizations within the sample who did not have the luxury of a large staff team with the time to develop an innovative and proactive funding strategy. It was explained by one of the activists within SICDP that the group was heavily reliant on the formal 'cold calling' approach and that it was generally remote from the funding community.

> Basically it is just going to known funders. There is a booklet out that you can get and you just [go through it]. What – – – did last year was just go through it and just mark off potential funders, that we would fit into their criteria and just write away, and there was a few we'd written off to [that] just came back, [saying] 'we don't fund things like that; we don't fund salaries, we don't fund running costs'. The way we would be looking at it [now, is that] we will have to go to funders that will give big funding. . . . We would be wanting no shorter than three years in funding so the commitment in big money would have to be there.[11]

Very few of the organizations surveyed would admit that they chased money by targeting a funder and designing a project that would fit into their funding criteria. Most preferred to characterize their strategy as being the reverse, namely developing their project and then searching for a funder whose criteria would be compatible with their initiative. The response of SICDP on this issue was typical of the majority of organizations surveyed during this research: 'Well, basically we're an established Project, so we know what we're going for. In our programme costs what we would do is form a strategy and then say, "Who would fund this?"'[12]

[11] Representative of the Springfield Inter-Community Development Project. Interview with authors, 13 August 1997.

[12] Ibid.

It is clear from this study that funding tends to have a snowballing nature in that the more successful a group becomes in attracting resources the easier the process becomes, while the small organizations on the fringes find it extremely difficult to gain access and establish their credibility within the funding community. The axiom that money begets money is an appropriate one with regard to funding patterns within the P/CRO sector, in that the larger organizations are good at sustaining themselves and becoming bigger, sucking up resources like business conglomerates, while the smaller groups find it more difficult to grow and quite often become smaller.

UCAN (Londonderry) are the epitome of the P/CRO at the bottom end of the scale, with an unevolved and basic strategy for acquiring resources. UCAN is not on a social network with the funding agencies, its main strategy being reactive, applying for funding in reaction to public announcements, filling in the relevant forms and generally having a formal and remote relationship to the funding community: 'For specific goals like conferences, we aim for the [local funding] groups, CRC. We don't have a strategy as such.'[13] Perhaps in an attempt to find triumph in adversity, one UCAN activist argued that they were happy not to have a close relationship with the core funding agencies. This suggestion was based on the logic that when an organization becomes friendly with its funders, it often becomes reliant on them and inevitably then becomes funding-oriented, thus running the risk of being vulnerable to the agenda of the funding agency and deflected from the original aims and objectives which the organization was set up to achieve. Typically, given the anti-elitist ethos that runs through groups such as UCAN, there is a certain pride in the achievements of the group despite the scarcity of resources, in comparison with the relatively 'richer' organizations that surround it. While it may be too strong to argue that they display 'nobility in poverty', there is a view that the work carried out by under-resourced groups such as theirs is of greater value than that generated by the fair-weather commitment of 'professional' community development workers within better resourced organizations. As one person put it: 'Most of this town [Londonderry] runs events that are completely

[13] Representative of UCAN (Londonderry). Interview with authors, 10 March 1997.

built around funding. If the funding wasn't there they would never have done it.'[14]

Some organizations faced structural problems with regard to their fundraising strategies due to the nature of their activities, their ideological focus and/or their public profile. FAIT for example (as explained above), while generally reactive rather than proactive in its approach, felt constrained by both the nature of its activity and the rules and legislation that governed the P/CRO sector. Aside from asking the British government (through the CCRU) to increase its core grant, the only form of fundraising activity engaged in by FAIT at the time of study (January 1997) was to send out written applications for donations to various organizations and companies. Due to the sensitive and highly political nature of their work, FAIT did not hold public fundraising events, nor did it have an active membership base to approach for donations. Those people who have used FAIT's services in a professional capacity are understandably anxious to maintain a low profile within the community. Aside from communicating with the CCRU there is little informal networking done to attract funding. The main approach, therefore, to private funding sources came in the form of a standard 'begging letter' to small-scale local businesses. This technique is extremely unsuccessful as most people in the business community were reluctant to give public (or even private) support to FAIT in case this either created difficulties amongst the staff working within their own organization or attracted attack from the paramilitaries. 'I would say [fear] is one of the main reasons [why such appeals are unsuccessful]. . . . We have received something like £600 in donations over the last twelve months. A journalist who was sympathetic to the organization and who just came to interview a couple of us here one day, gave us £80, so what's that? That's roughly about 18 per cent of our annual donations.'[15] In addition to the nervousness of potential private donors, FAIT believed that the rules on NGO funding prevented the group from acquiring charitable status because of the political nature of their work, thus depriving them of much-needed resources.

14 Ibid. 13 April 1997.

15 Representative of FAIT. Interview with authors, 28 November 1996.

> Charitable status is one of our big blocks. In one particular case about two years ago, there was a very wealthy Irish American who promised us $10,000, but when we told him that we didn't have charitable status, it prevented him from giving us that money. I would say that if we had charitable status we would get a lot more money from America.[16]

Women Together is typical of the mid- to small-sized P/CRO in Northern Ireland, in that its members realize the importance of putting a coherent fundraising strategy in place but do not have the resources available to allocate organizational energy to it, with most of the burden falling on the co-ordinator – who also has to deal with all the other main organizational functions such as recruitment, accounting, media work and so on. The devising and implementing of a long-term funding strategy can easily be neglected, therefore, due to more pressing priorities. Like many P/CROs, Women Together generates some income internally through annual subscriptions. However, these are usually a small fraction of the overall budget and are kept deliberately low to avoid potential members feeling excluded because of their economic circumstances (£2 unwaged, £5 waged in the case of Women Together when surveyed in 1997). Women Together welcomes donations, while activists in the organization also hold various fundraising events from time to time and raise small amounts of money locally.

> We are actually this year [1997] looking at organizing a summer event and an autumn event. . . . We also have gathered together quite a few T-shirts with signatures of various famous people on them, and we are going to have an auction at some stage. That would be ongoing [fundraising activity] but it is finding the time to do that sort of thing, it takes a lot of organization and we are looking for a lot of members to help in that respect.[17]

Like many other mid-sized P/CROs studied, Women Together have a much closer relationship with local funders than they do with those from outside Northern Ireland, and feel that they are on a social network with the core funder, the Community Relations Council. They could phone up and talk to the funder on a first-name basis in a relatively relaxed and informal atmosphere. This would also be true

16 Ibid.

17 Representative of Women Together for Peace. Interview with authors, 5 May 1997.

of other funders such as the government's Central Community Relations Unit (CCRU) and the Ireland Funds. These are funders who know Women Together and with whom the organization has built up a relationship. There are other funders such as the private trusts and foundations that Women Together do not have a close or informal relationship with.

Many P/CROs recognize the importance of building up social networks within the funding community and are keen to move away from simple 'paper applications' that keep the group at a distance from the funder. The funding strategy pursued by the Clogher Valley Rural Development Centre epitomizes this attempt by the P/CRO sector to sell their projects more proactively and vigorously to potential donors. A representative from the group explained their approach:

> I think I get on with the [funders] fine. [We] simply bring them down, invite them in, show them around, tell them what we're trying to do and they say, 'No, we don't do that; we don't fund that,' [Then] we say, 'Well, what will you fund?' Then we'll talk to them about what they can fund, what was in their remit, and then we will try to sell the project to them, or if they say no, they won't fund that, we'll say, 'Well, why not?' And they'll say, 'Because it doesn't have A, B or C,' and we'll say, 'Right, but if we put that [there] and did this . . . would that not sort of constitute an A, B and C?' . . . It's only when you come down and look out the windows . . . and you chat to people [about] what you do and you take them round and you show them the different groups that use this place, only then, I think, [do] they get a feel of what the place is about.[18]

As the above shows, the Centre's strategy for attracting funding is informal to start with, and includes where possible establishing personal contact with the funder, getting a feel for what their funding criteria are and whether the group meets these criteria, and what they would be likely to fund if not the project which the Centre had in mind. They would then submit a formal application when both sides have already had some form of contact.

Larger P/CRO groups, such as the Committee on the Administration of Justice, illustrate a much more proactive and organized funding strategy. This group is at the opposite end of the spectrum to the smaller P/CROs such as UCAN (Londonderry), in having a much more coherent and knowledgeable sense of the funding universe and

[18] Representative of the Clogher Valley Rural Development Centre. Interview with authors, 20 May 1997.

in being much better connected to it. This was partly a consequence of spending more time on developing its funding strategy, together with being able to utilize more internally generated resources. A representative from the organization illustrated the different ways in which the group attempted to maximize its funding:

> We've a variety of ways in which we try to raise money. One is we bring money in from publications. So we try to promote our publications and increase the income that we bring in from publications. We bring some money in from membership and try to increase the number of members. . . . We bring some money in now through training which we offer to people; it's a small proportion of income but if we do a workshop for a trade union we would expect the trade union then to pay us for doing that. . . . We raise money through foundations, locally, nationally and internationally. . . . That [involves] basically the traditional kind of fundraising skills, working out who's got the money [and] trying to work out how to get them to give you it.[19]

An example of the proactive and innovative funding strategy of the CAJ is provided by its attempt to generate a substantial income by establishing an endowment. This was seen as a means of combating the inevitable planning problems associated with short-term funding and insulating the organization from criticism concerning its independence.

> That seems to us to deal with a number of problems in one go. One is that it means that they [critics] can't question your independence any more, they can't say, 'Well, you got this money to do that piece of research and that came from that Trade Union, and as a result of that, this is why you've come up with these kind of arguments, or it came from that Foundation and they're supported by such and such.' So it seems to us that if we could raise a general large amount of money in order to establish an endowment, that solves the problem about charges of not being independent. It also solves the problem of long-term stability and it gives you a situation where you know that each year you're going to have this amount of money, and that means then that you can plan better. So that's the kind of money we would like, and that would be our preferred option in terms of funding.[20]

The interviewee was asked to describe how this relationship operated in practice. Did the CAJ devise a project, ring up a contact in a

[19] Representative of the Committee on the Administration of Justice. Interview with authors, 26 May 1997.

[20] Ibid.

funding agency with whom they would be on first name terms, outline the project to them and ask whether they would be eligible to apply formally for funding?

> Yes, I mean I would have over my period of time working here and through the other work that I have done, I would have developed a fairly extensive network of people who I know have money to give to certain things. We would perhaps be planning a particular piece of work and we would decide that we would need to raise specific funds in order to do that, and I would draw upon the network of people who I know and perhaps consider making applications to some of those people, phoning them up first, sounding them out, saying, you know, 'Would this be something that you could do?' Asking their advice as to whether, if this was something they couldn't do, who else might, and then more generally, you know, looking through books like the *Guide to Major Trusts* and trying to identify possible sources from that. So a lot of it is personal contact and certainly, yes, I would know the people who fund us; yes, I could call up [and have an informal discussion].[21]

It was pointed out that this strategy was seen as a means of making the formal application more attractive to the funder rather than 'cold calling' them, or simply making a formal written approach. This allowed the P/CRO to do their 'homework' and refine the formal application from a position of strength. Such preliminary contacts can help to determine, for example, whether or not it is worth making an application in the first place, thus reducing organizational effort in chasing lost causes. If such informal discussions convince the P/CRO that a formal approach for funding might be considered, they could also help the group to assess what kinds of emphasis should be placed on different aspects of the application. This technique was ably explained by one of the P/CROs in the sample, which has been relatively successful in building up a long-term funding strategy:

> For example, we might want to organize a conference and that conference might have a cross-border dimension; it might have a dimension of bringing in participants from excluded groups and it might have, at the end of it, a publication which is going to come out of it. So in order to do all of that the conference is going to cost £10,000. Now, on phoning some of these people they might say, 'Well you know, the only bit of that we can do is the publication', or, 'The only bit of that we could do is the cross-border bit and we could fund the publication for you, but I can't

[21] Ibid.

> help to subsidize the travel for the people coming from Dublin'. So that's a direction, in a sense, which they're giving you, so when you're writing that application you spend more time talking about the dimension that they're likely to support and you put together [the application accordingly]. So some of the things that we do are supported by one trust, some of them are supported by five trusts, you know.[22]

The P/CROs which indulged in this indirect funding strategy as a complement to the more formal procedures were the larger organizations with more extensive social networks; they were, in general, more successful at fundraising than those who took the view that 'small (and poor) is beautiful' and those who adopted a more reactive and remote position from the funding community.

Forbidden funding

Aside from the amount of funding P/CROs can acquire, they also face a number of potential ethical questions concerning the sources of their revenue. In general, there appeared to be few ethical dilemmas with regard to funding, despite the fact that most of the P/CROs in Northern Ireland are effectively 'bank rolled' at some level by the British government. For most groups it seems to be a practical issue. How can the organization generate sufficient resources to maintain its existing work and develop new projects without taking money that will compromise its integrity, damage its credibility and thus inhibit it from operating effectively?

Ethical issues fall into two broad categories: first, sources that may be questionable in terms of the P/CRO's general ideological ethos, such as right-wing foundations or businesses with links to the arms or gambling industries; second, sources that impact more directly on the political ideology of the P/CRO, and/or public perceptions of the donor as being a party to the conflict (even if only at several removes) with a corresponding belief that funding from such sources is 'dirty money' or in more extreme cases, 'blood money'. Most of the groups studied in the course of this research took a very pragmatic view of these ethical problems and in general did not have clear and explicit policies on the sources of funding that the organization would view as 'forbidden'. This was largely because the problem had not arisen

22 Ibid.

for many P/CROs, with most groups concentrating on the well-known local, British, Irish, European and international funders, rather than searching out more exotic sources more likely to present such ethical problems.

For most of the groups few limitations were imposed by the first general category. When an activist within one of the smaller community development organizations was asked whether the organization would accept funding from a tobacco company, it was suggested facetiously that they would 'take drugs money!' A similar response came from a member of the Clogher Valley Rural Development Centre, who remarked, 'No, I'd take anybody's money. . . . Well, anybody's money within reason I suppose, but when you're trying to promote economic development and community relations and community development, it doesn't matter a damn to me who pays for the photocopier, you know?'[23]

The second category of funding was often more problematic as it could be regarded as being 'political' funding and could potentially conflict with the organizational ethos of the P/CRO or damage their public profile. The following example provides a good illustration of the ethical difficulties faced by some groups, and the pragmatic approach that is often taken. A representative from the radical loyalist UCAN (Londonderry) was asked if they would accept money from the International Fund for Ireland (IFI). In the past, many loyalist groups saw this funding as being part of the Anglo-Irish Agreement, and thus as a bribe to encourage acceptance of a policy with which they disagreed. In the wake of the signing of the Anglo-Irish Agreement in November 1985, the general unionist community was encouraged by several unionist politicians to shun the IFI. It became clear that this source was not an important ethical consideration for UCAN (Londonderry) when the matter was discussed in 1997, and that the focus was on the practical benefits that funding could bring to the community. 'To tell you the honest truth, the job is more important. . . . If there is a need and there is money, take it.'[24]

[23] Representative of the Clogher Valley Rural Development Centre. Interview with authors, 28 May 1997.

[24] Representative of UCAN (Londonderry). Interview with authors, 10 March 1997.

Another community development group within Northern Ireland with strong links within the loyalist community is the Springfield Inter-Community Development Project. This scheme was originally core funded by the IFI. When one of the group's founders was asked whether this funding source presented ethical difficulties for the organization, either internally or among the wider loyalist community, the explanation was based upon a pragmatic outlook of how it could be used, rather than any doctrinaire sense that the money was politically 'tainted'.

> When IFI funded us we just went ahead with the funding even though on the unionist side it's perceived as Irish-based money, but we went ahead with it and took their money because it was for the benefit of the community. . . . It [the source of the funding] was never brought up, it was just accepted that this Project had been born and that Billy [Hutchinson] was being established in the local community and he was very much respected, and actually, where his wages came from, I don't think was an issue.[25]

Interestingly, one of the most sophisticated P/CROs in the sample with regard to the ethics of funding was the Committee on the Administration of Justice. While they are a cross-community human rights organization, they are more fastidious than some republican groups about taking funding from British government sources. They are explicit in their refusal to accept government funding. This does not come from an ideological position on the constitutional debate, but more from a concern to protect the independence and integrity of the organization. The CAJ, in other words, not only wishes to guard its independence, but also wants this independence to be transparent, given the context of their human rights work. Unlike most of the other groups surveyed during this research, the CAJ have had to think carefully about this issue, due in part to the fact that they have a much more complex funding structure than many of the other organizations. A representative from the CAJ explained the group's policy on the ethics of funding in the following way:

> If somebody gave us money and sought to have undue control over the outcome of that, [if] they said, 'Right, we'd like you to do a piece of

25 Representative of the Springfield Inter-Community Development Project. Interview with authors, 9 December 1997.

> research on policing, but the recommendations that you publish we'd have to see'. We'd say no to that. So money that seeks to tie us to a particular outcome or to give external people particular control over what we do we would refuse, and I guess there would be situations where, for example, some company that's involved in the arms trade would offer us [funding and that would be unacceptable]. . . . We have a little flow chart; it's got the nature of the work along the top and the nature of the funding [along the side] and it looks at whether the funding is good. . . . And there is a matrix . . . it's got little tick boxes or question marks, and the general [idea is], is this likely to bring the organization into disrepute? Is it likely to, you know [damage the group's credibility?]. They are modelled on principles that Amnesty International apply.[26]

The CAJ sees an important distinction in the way funding is used within the organization and would differentiate between the core costs of the group and project-related funding associated with one-off pieces of work. The funding of non-contentious work such as administrative support could use sources not used to finance work designed to influence policy or projects with a substantial human rights focus. The key issue for the CAJ in terms of accepting funding is how this relates to the central human rights ethos of the organization. If the ethical questions posed by the funder are linked to issues of human rights or civil liberties (such as a business with links to the arms industry), then they would clearly be unacceptable sources of financial support. They would be rejected on moral grounds, but also on pragmatic grounds, as this would risk the credibility of the CAJ as a campaigning organization on human rights issues. The position is more complicated where the ethical questions are subsidiary to the central focus of the CAJ, as in the case of the British National Lottery, which some groups oppose on religious grounds for encouraging gambling, and others object to because of the effects it has on the poorest sections of society. Accepting Lottery money would not necessarily be seen as morally repugnant, and in pragmatic terms would not damage the credibility of the CAJ greatly. 'I think the best way to describe the approach is that [we] would make some assessment as to whether taking this money is likely to bring the organization into disrepute, likely to hinder the effective realization of its goals, is likely to get in the way of what we're trying to do, so a

[26] Representative of the Committee on the Administration of Justice. Interview with authors, 6 June 1997.

whole variety of things could come under that, where it could be the control issue, or the perception of control.'[27]

While Dove House Resource Centre (a community development group that deals mainly with those from within the nationalist/ republican community) might be expected to have greater ethical difficulties in accepting funding from the British government than P/CROs such as the CAJ, this was not the case. A member of the organization was asked whether accepting funding from British government sources such as the Training and Employment Agency (T&EA) or the Northern Ireland Voluntary Trust (NIVT), was problematic, given both the personal political attitudes of most of those involved with Dove House, and the organization's opposition to British government policy on issues such as contested parades by the Orange Order and Apprentice Boys of Derry? The response was that the organization had no difficulty accepting British government money from such sources. However, there was one funding source from which money would be forbidden. That was the Prince's Trust charity [a charitable organization established by the Prince of Wales]. The reason given was that such money would be unacceptable because of Prince Charles's ceremonial leadership of the paratroop regiment of the British army, the regiment responsible for killing fourteen unarmed civilians in Derry in 1972 (Bloody Sunday). Aside from this, there were few sources of funding that would be unacceptable to Dove House.

It is curious that a single-identity group such as Dove House Resource Centre appears to have more latitude over the ethics of its funding sources than organizations such as the CAJ. Perhaps the reason for this relates to the cohesion of its support base. The ideological ethos of Dove House and its largely republican participation profile, mean that there is little risk of the organization being accused of following a British government agenda, simply because it accepted funding from state agencies such as the T&EA. This, together with the fact that community development work is less 'risky' to fund than human rights activity, may explain why the CAJ has to be more cautious about it donors.

It is clear that for Dove House, as for most other P/CROs examined during the course of this research, the source of funding is a prag-

[27] Ibid.

matic rather than an ideological issue. It is interesting that debates on funding were more likely to occur over practical matters such as the value of the ACE programme [a government scheme designed to provide unemployed people with one year's employment on low wages, paid for by the government instead of the employer], rather than ideological points such as the question of 'dirty' money. While many of those in the P/CROs studied, particularly community development groups top-heavy with programmes and activities, were enthusiastic about the T&EA's funding of the ACE scheme, as it provided the organizations with workers they could not afford to pay at the normal commercial rates, the scheme was not universally welcomed within Dove House, with one activist blaming it for 'mission drift' within the organization. This refers to an issue highlighted in the previous chapter, namely the internal difficulties faced by P/CRO as they evolve and change over time and as their institutional development impacts upon (or appears to impact on) the focus and activities of the group:

> . . . I think that Dove House was at its most successful when it dealt with self-help issues. Once it got into ACE funding, it became a different sort of organization, and a less successful organization. You will hear lot of people in the so-called 'voluntary sector' talking about how tragic it is that ACE has been lost. [I think] ACE was an awful system of workfare that didn't aid unemployment, didn't provide people with great skills, and was just cheap labour basically, and cheap labour which tied groups like Dove House, and other groups, into an administrative system, which actually diffused the energy and the potential creativity to address some of the problems people were having. . . . I think that whenever the senior personnel were put into core-funded posts and then had additional responsibilities for administering the wages and the general administration, . . . that that took away from the potential to address problems as and when they arose on an immediate day-to-day basis. It slowed down the response [time] and it also lost [the] focus of where Dove House had originally set up to go. . . . So, it became an organization that was simply there to perpetuate its own existence, and I think that ACE was the primary reason for that. . . . If you looked at societies for the prevention of cruelty to animals, what they do now is [to] put down dogs. They [neuter] cats. Could you imagine anything more cruel than chopping the goolies off a cat? So, it almost got to the stage where Dove House was doing things because they were forced down a path, to secure funding, (which was necessary). . . . Dove House had become a kind of ACE project. . . . The intention would be to try and reinvent Dove House, and take it back almost to where it started. Now, whether we can do that is another question, because in the minds of local people,

> Dove House is now a nice friendly place where, if you are on the dole for a year and you are looking for another few pound extra, you go and ask Dove House to see if there are any ACE jobs coming up. It will take a lot of time to try and change that. In order to get a radical edge on things, it doesn't take any more than three or four people.[28]

P/CRO relationships with funders

The majority of P/CROs looked at had a relatively relaxed operational relationship with their main funders. While reporting procedures were formal, there was often a degree of communication beyond this between donor and recipient that allowed the funder to act in an advisory capacity as required, while remaining informed of the group's activities. An activist within the CAJ (one of the larger groups examined) explained it in the following terms: 'The relationship with our funders is good and is constantly maintained. I mean we get money from people because they like what we do, they respect what we do and we have a good relationship with all the people who fund us.'[29]

Accountability procedures are normally very formal between the P/CROs and funders, though the precise demands may vary from one organization to another. One funder will require quarterly reports while another will want the P/CRO to send the annual report and to submit another report midway through the grant cycle. Some funders may want to visit the group to talk about the grant application or the progress of work it is already funding, while others may demand to see the minutes of committee meetings to determine whether the organization is being run efficiently. However, this last option is rarely used and is more likely to be applied in the case of a smaller organization with few staff, than large P/CRO with a proven track record and more formalized employment and financial procedures. The usual pattern would be the submission of audited accounts either quarterly or annually, together with periodic progress reports detailing the work that was being done. The example of Women Together is typical. It provides its core funder with an annual report

[28] Representative of Dove House Resource Centre. Interview with authors, 9 October 1997.

[29] Representative of the Committee on the Administration of Justice. Interview with authors, 6 June 1997.

and a six-monthly report, together with its quarterly newsletters. If they receive extra funding for a particular project, they provide the funder with a six-monthly update of how the project is progressing, whether it is completed, how successful it is, and if it is ongoing, what the next stage is. They also supply monthly bank statements and submit financial reports to show the funder that the money is actually being spent on the purpose it was intended for. As one representative put it, 'The whole thing is quite carefully controlled'.[30]

Few of the organizations studied had experienced poor relationships with the funding community, beyond feeling that they were underfunded. However, some expressed annoyance that the particular interpretation of a funder's remit had prevented them from applying to it for resources, or would have required them to change the focus of their activities and reconstitute organizational structures in order to do so. In the cases where this did occur, it was believed that the motivation was accidental (naivety about the organizational ethos) rather than a deliberate attempt to pressurize the P/CRO or engineer a fundamental change in its strategic direction, ideological focus or core activities. However, one case is different from the others studied. Dove House Resource Centre believes it was the victim of 'political vetting' in 1986, which resulted in its core funding being stopped by the Training and Employment Agency (T&EA). This was perceived by the organization to be a consequence of the Hurd principles [after former British Foreign Secretary, Douglas Hurd], which stated that government money should not be given to organizations in Northern Ireland that were 'fronts' for 'terrorist groups' or that gave support to 'terrorist groups'. Dove House was not charged with any specific allegations in this regard, but its funding was stopped in 1986 with no reason given. It would be reasonable to assume that this was a political decision, as the funding was restored and increased by the T&EA the following year and the ACE workers actually increased from four to twelve shortly after the decision was reversed. A representative from Dove House explained the background to this situation and how the group responded to it:

[30] Representative of Women Together for Peace. Interview with authors, 13 March 1997.

> Actually what happened was that vetting came about as a result of the statement that Douglas Hurd made in the House of Commons in 1985. It was first implemented against Conway Mill in Belfast and Springhill House. Dove House actually supported those community organizations and lent that support publicly. [Then Dove House] got the formal NIO [Northern Ireland Office] letter telling them that their funding was also being removed. Now, the management committee at the time [began] a public campaign to have the funding restored and [get] an apology to the members of the [management] committee. The funding was actually restored in September 1986, but no apology, and there was no explanation given for why it was removed in the first place or why it was restored in the second place.[31]

Dove House launched a campaign to have the group's funding restored and this was supported by influential leaders within the community such as John Hume (leader of the SDLP), Bishop Edward Daly, the local Catholic Church leader, and Derry City Council. This eventually led to international support from the United States and pressure on the British government to reverse its decision.

Typically, concern over political vetting is highest within single-identity working-class organizations primarily engaged in community development activity, rather than cross-community groups with a more overt peace and reconciliation focus. This episode illustrates the fine line that some P/CROs tread with regard to how they are likely to be perceived within the minds of funders (or those who direct them) with respect to whether they are engaged in resolving community conflict or actually helping to create and perpetuate it. (See Chapter 7 for a more detailed discussion of the impact of single-identity groups on the resolution of conflict in Northern Ireland.)

The Dove House episode is also symptomatic of a wider issue concerning the whole P/CRO sector and the general relationship between these organizations and the funding community. This is that *trust* is the crucial ingredient in the partnership between donor and recipient. If this breaks down, either because of inadequate auditing structures, financial irregularities, unsatisfactory progress of work, or the belief of the funder that resources are being used to fund other activities than those they were given to support, then inevitably the whole relationship between the P/CRO and the funder

31 Representative of Dove House Resource Centre. Interview with authors, 17 September 1997.

will be seriously damaged. Gaining and maintaining the trust of the funder is the key to an effective funding strategy. The successful P/CRO will be the one that has a track-record of stability; the reputation for delivering services efficiently, or campaigning energetically and effectively; personnel who are known and respected by the funders; and that generally creates the impression within the funding community that the group has the staff and organizational structure to carry out what it says it will do, that no other group could do the same thing better than the one being funded, and that there is little risk to the funder of the money being misused.

It could be argued, of course, that the side effects of this trend are not altogether beneficial. It places the emphasis not on the *ideas* put forward for P/CR initiatives, but instead gives primacy (albeit indirectly) to the organizations that promote them. There may well be a bias, therefore, in favour of funding the 'moderate', 'safe', middle-class, established group that pursues an ethos similar to that of the funder but fails to confront the really difficult and controversial issues at the heart of the political conflict in Northern Ireland. Groups that are considered to be a greater 'risk' to fund, that are not connected by a social network to the funders, that have no track record, and that perhaps take a more critical approach to peace/conflict resolution activity, may therefore be crowded out by the understandable concern of the funding community to maintain existing support for the more traditional and experienced organizations.

This issue of P/CRO effectiveness lies at the heart of this research study and will be examined in the next chapter.

7

Hitting the Target or Firing Blanks? The Impact of P/CROs on the Peace Process in Northern Ireland

This chapter has been compiled with the help of a series of interviews with key players in civil society, including funders, practitioners, politicians, academics and journalists. The narrative will distil the central arguments expressed by the interviewees concerning the impact of P/CROs on the 'peace process', and provide a critical analysis of the P/CRO sector.[1]

[1] As some of the interviewees wish their contributions to remain anonymous, none of the sources will be attributed for the sake of consistency. However, we would like to thank the following people for their assistance in the compilation of this part of the book: Sean Farren (SDLP); Avila Kilmurray (NIVT); Marie Mullholland (Women's Support Network); Dennis McCoy (Formerly of NISRA); Paul Sweeney (formerly of the District Partnership Board); Derek Wilson (University of Ulster); Robin Wilson (Democratic Dialogue). Formal interviews were carried out with respondents from different areas within civil society. These interviews were relatively long (between one and three hours) and sometimes extended to multiple sessions. The interviewees were all highly influential in their respective areas and a selection was made across the relevant fields of journalism, academia, the civil service, politics, and the voluntary and community sector outside the scope of the project.

One of the interviewees (SDLP politician, Sean Farren) was directly involved in the political negotiations at Stormont and has since been elected to the Northern Ireland Assembly and the Northern Ireland Executive as Minister for Further and Higher Education. However, political access for most of the P/CROs sampled was limited, though some informal lobbying did take place between some of the human rights groups such as the CAJ and FAIT, of local politicians, government officials and ministers.

In view of the energy and resources which P/CROs devote to dealing with aspects of the conflict in Northern Ireland, it seems sensible to try to establish the overall impact and effect which this effort has had (is having) on the 'peace process'. Actually doing this is extremely difficult in practical terms. How do we *measure* the effectiveness of peace and conflict resolution organizations? Do we compare the amount of work that is going on with the increase in peace and conflict resolution that has occurred in a given period? Clearly this measurement of 'peace by the yard' is an inadequate methodological basis, which will yield information of little value.

In reality, much of the most useful activity in this field is conducted invisibly and is not tied to particular events; it is often not appreciable when it is carried out, its value only becoming apparent in combination with other events and actions when viewed over time. Consequently, it is impossible to measure the impact of P/CROs quantitatively, other than in the most basic of terms. The alternative is to give a qualitative assessment of the impact of the P/CRO sector over the last thirty years of political conflict in Northern Ireland. This is, by its very nature, impressionistic rather than definitive. However, it will at least bring together the main arguments of advocates and critics alike, and stimulate what is a necessary debate as the resources that are available to the sector begin to decline. Have P/CROs changed the terms of political debate? Has their work influenced our political vocabulary and the way in which most people view the conflict in Northern Ireland? More fundamentally perhaps, would society look any different today if the P/CRO sector had not existed

More importantly, reflecting a point made later in this chapter concerning the movement of NGO personnel into politics in the 1990s, some of those involved in groups such as the Springfield Inter-Community Development Project, Women Together for Peace, the Ulster People's College, and the Peace Train, have become directly involved in the political process and in the negotiations leading to the signing of the Good Friday Agreement on 10 April 1998.

While care would be taken by such individuals to make a distinction between their political activity and their community development and conflict resolution work, there is an inevitable link between the two, even if this is only in terms of how they are perceived by those outside their organizations.

The interviews were carried out between October 1997 and March 1998.

for the last thirty years? These are some of the questions that will be addressed in this chapter.

Good works versus power politics

One way of trying to assess the effect of P/CROs on politics in Northern Ireland is by determining the most important events that have occurred over the last thirty years, which people believe have led to the calling of the republican and loyalist ceasefires and eventually to the Good Friday Agreement of April 1998. If the work of the P/CRO sector is cited as having been important in the context of the 'peace process', then this would clearly substantiate the argument that such organizations had exerted some effect and influence. However, as one interviewee remarked when asked to select a number of significant events that have led Northern Ireland towards a new political dispensation: 'I find it difficult to disentangle [the concepts within the questions]. . . . It might be difficult to disentangle simply because everything blends into everything else, and what is very significant at any one moment, may in the overall [picture] appear much less significant.'[2]

In fact, notwithstanding the general difficulty in selecting a handful of significant events over a thirty-year period, no one who was interviewed on this subject mentioned the activity of the P/CRO sector as being of fundamental importance to the peace process. Perhaps the most interesting finding was that in addition to a range of political initiatives, many people pointed to a number of violent events as being benchmarks in bringing Northern Ireland further along the road to peace. One commentator put it like this:

> There have been so many, and when I look back in trying to identify significant events that have made a contribution to peace, I mean some of them, I suppose, have to be the terrible events in the run-up to the declaration of the ceasefires [1994]; the Shankill bombings and all of those [October 1993], maybe gave an urgency to things, but would the declarations of ceasefires in '94 have happened anyway? I think they were in somebody's sights at that stage. They were going to happen in my view, because the initiatives that precipitated them had been going on for a period, and they were coming to culmination, and the work of

[2] Off-the-record interview with authors, 12 February 1998.

> the two governments and of various contacts were pushing them in that direction.[3]

It was further argued that the role of the P/CRO sector was not to lead the political process from the front, but that its effect has been subliminal, making visible what would otherwise be invisible, and providing an outlet for the expression of public opinion.

> In a sense, you could say that the continual demonstration, either in a very demonstrative way, like the Peace People's rallies, or other similar events throughout the three decades of violence, signalled that there was a considerable section of the community [who were] totally opposed to violence, and there was always a rein on terrorism and on those who went for the violent option. To that you add the fact that we did have the expressions of democratic options through the ballot box, again demonstrating very clearly that people were not, in any significant way, behind the violence. So I suppose you might boil it down in one way to the good sense of the people of Northern Ireland, that they did not want to go over the precipice, they wanted to pull back and they were looking for the leadership that would pull them back.[4]

This view, that the mere existence of the P/CRO sector was beneficial regardless of any empirically definable achievements, is unimpressive. It epitomizes the woolly liberalism and well-meaning but ultimately ineffectual culture for which the sector has rightly been criticized. Considering the degree of public money that has poured into the P/CRO 'industry' over the last thirty years, its defenders should be able to come up with more than a 'better than nothing' advocacy to justify its existence.

There is, for example, a strong case to be made that the activity of P/CROs has been entirely incidental to the peace process and that political progress in Northern Ireland has instead been determined by those in positions of power and influence, namely, the politicians and the paramilitaries. This view was put forward in a strident fashion by a political commentator interviewed during the course of this research. This individual suggested that the dynamics behind the ceasefires and subsequent political negotiations, were *because of*, rather than *in spite of*, the level of communal polarization, and had little to do with the progressive thinking or positive work of the P/CRO sector. It was argued that the peace process was only possible

[3] Ibid.
[4] Ibid.

due to the engineering of paramilitary doublethink, where republicans were only able to sign up to it on the basis of a belief that they could prosecute their objectives politically via the cultivation of the 'nationalist consensus' [i.e. a broad coalition between Sinn Fein, the SDLP and the Irish government], while the loyalists bought into it because they thought that the union with Britain was secure and would not be diluted. This observer believed that the major political dynamics in Northern Ireland were not governed by NGOs or P/CROs but by the interaction of paramilitary organizations with the *realpolitik* agenda of the policy-makers. Ironically, it was *politically motivated violence* that had produced the momentum for peace, rather than the activities of the P/CRO sector. The Shankill and Greysteel killings of 1993, for example, had produced the dynamic for the Six Spring Principles for Peace that evolved into the Downing Street Declaration of December 1993.

> Sure, there is no question about that. I think one of the big problems about resolving the conflict is that a number of signals have been sent out over the years, to both sets of paramilitaries, that violence in some sense pays, or at least sets the agenda, and government itself has never got its human rights act together in such a way as to be able to say that its own hands are completely clean in that regard. There have been enough things that government has done or presided over, over the years, whether it is the shoot-to-kill controversies or going back to 'Bloody Sunday' or whatever, to make it difficult for government to have assumed an effective high moral ground against violence. And in practice on many occasions it has been evident that violence has set the agenda. . . . There have been numerous occasions in terms of loyalism, most obviously, the Ulster Workers Council Strike [1974], where force has been deployed, [also] the Drumcree mobilization, in such a way as to persuade the Catholic community that that will always be what trumps any political development, unless that is faced down. . . . So yes, I think one of the real difficulties over the years is that whereas the NGOs who have been involved have often tended to represent a kind of ethical perspective as to what should be [done] in terms of values – values of human rights, values of reconciliation, values of justice, values of peace, etc. – the difficulty is that government has usually worked simply with a short-term *realpolitik,* in response to events, particularly violent events like the Shankill and Greysteel, which has meant that it has been unable to hold the high moral ground in any real sense and, in fact, has constantly had to respond to this or that pressure, threat or violent activity, in such a way that while it makes expedient sense at the time, it has tended to corrode the credibility of democratic values over time.[5]

[5] Off-the-record interview with authors, 10 March 1998.

Many of those interviewed on this issue pointed to the Shankill bombing and Greysteel shootings of October and November 1993, as significant events on the road to the peace process. This created a climate in the autumn of 1993 that left many feeling that the only alternative to a reinvigorated political progress, was a downward spiral of politically motivated violence that would lead ultimately to civil war. This 'last chance saloon' presented by Shankill and Greysteel concentrated the minds of people in Northern Ireland to fill the political vacuum with a credible political process.

One observer remarked that while it may be an unpalatable truth for P/CRO activists to contemplate, the real dynamics behind political progress lay not in the 'good works' of individuals within that sector, but rather were to be found in the balance-sheet mentalities of the protagonists to the conflict. Put bluntly, the most important event that led to the creation of the Northern Ireland peace process was when Sinn Féin President Gerry Adams changed his mind and formed the opinion that the 'armed struggle' would not achieve republican objectives without a significant new political initiative. From this perspective, the events that followed this epiphany were driven, not by pressure applied through the work of peace and reconciliation groups, but by a desire on the part of key individuals within the republican leadership to reposition Sinn Féin politically. Within this scenario the activity of the P/CRO sector was at best marginal in its impact on the macro-political environment.

It was also pointed out, however, that the one big unequivocal success story of the P/CRO sector was provided by the growth of integrated education in Northern Ireland and the ability of its advocates to bring about a significant change in government policy towards integrated education. It was suggested that this alternative sector has worked to the extent that it is growing in size and is offering an alternative ethos that people have the opportunity of buying into, which is genuinely multicultural. The impact of integrated education on social and political attitudes in Northern Ireland is a subject of some debate.[6] While this is a sector of education provision that has

[6] See in particular G. Fraser and V. Morgan, *In the Frame – Integrated Education in Northern Ireland: The Implications of Expansion* (Coleraine: Centre for the Study of Conflict, 1999); V. Morgan, S. Dunn, E. Cairns and G. Fraser, *Breaking the Mould: The Roles of Parents and Teachers in Integrated Schools in Northern Ireland* (Coleraine: Centre for the Study of Conflict, 1992); A.

expanded quickly over the last ten years, its qualitative impact on sectarian attitudes in Northern Ireland is difficult to assess. It is fair to say that the P/CRO sector has been successful in promoting integrated education and that this has led to a rapid expansion in the level of its provision at both primary and secondary levels. What is not clear, however, is the extent to which this success in augmenting the number of integrated schools has been paralleled in the social and political attitudes of the pupils who have attended them. Leading researchers in the field paint a broadly positive picture of integrated education, but are far from sanguine about its social and political impact on Northern Ireland.

> The number of integrated schools has quadrupled between 1989 and 1997. Most significantly the number of integrated secondary level schools has increased from 2 in 1990 to 14 in 1997. At the same time overall enrolments have increased from under 2,000 in 1991 to about 7,000 in 1996. Though to insert a note of caution, this figure represents a little over 2% of the total Northern Ireland school population. For those parents seeking an alternative outside the established dual system and for the large number of activists who have contributed enormous amounts of time and energy into founding schools and establishing support structures all this represents a significant achievement.[7]

> At a structural level the segregation within the education system in Northern Ireland appears to be resistant to change. Most children continue to be educated in predominantly Catholic or Protestant schools and equity issues tend to be addressed in terms of these two blocks. However, the past twenty years have also brought new types of school which, despite their small numbers, introduce a potential for change and raise questions about the overall administration and control of education within the society.[8]

A number of people interviewed during the course of this research cited Initiative '92/the Opsahl Commission on Northern Ireland, as one of the earliest examples of an attempt to establish an inclusive political dialogue, and saw this as an important stepping stone to the eventual move towards inclusive all-party talks at the élite level.

Montgomery and A. Smith, *Values in Education in Northern Ireland* (Belfast: CCEA, 1997).

7 G. Fraser and V. Morgan (1999), p. 2.

8 Alan Smith, (School of Education, University of Ulster, Northern Ireland), 'Education and the Peace Process in Northern Ireland', Paper presented to the Annual Conference of the American Education Research Association, Montreal, April 1999.

> I think the Opsahl Commission created a climate in terms of people saying that groups must engage and we must be actually looking at some level of compromise and that the absolutes must be broken down. I think Opsahl was also important for very clearly reaching out in terms of speaking to republicans and loyalists and trying to break down some of the stereotypes.[9]

It was also claimed that this presented a conflict resolution strategy that went beyond the formal political process and involved civil society in a more holistic manner. 'I think the biggest thing that has happened since the early '90s, although not always accepted or recognized, is the fact that we've moved away from the central philosophy that it is up to the centre parties to sort things out.'[10] One interviewee who was a co-founder of Initiative '92 and the Opsahl Commission, claimed that these examples of P/CRO activity did have a positive influence on the political process, particularly at government level. Senior policy-makers began talking in 1995 about establishing an 'Opsahl-type' forum as part of a new round of talks between the parties. This was envisaged as being a body that would augment the traditional political process by taking evidence from people and acting as a sounding board for ideas within wider public opinion. While this bore little resemblance to the Northern Ireland Forum, which was eventually established in 1996, it did suggest that the Opsahl Report, and the culture of inclusiveness and dialogue that informed this initiative, had some impact on thinking at government level. It would also be fair to conclude that the subsequent provision for the Civic Forum as part of the Good Friday Agreement owes its antecedents (in part at least) to the Opsahl Commission that preceded it.

Clearly, equations of cause and effect are difficult to establish when it comes to assessing the impact of P/CROs on the peace process. The chain of events is a complex one, as is the very terminology that surrounds it. As astutely pointed out by one commentator, determining a logic to this chain of events was difficult as it was impossible to isolate or decontextualize the political conflict. The very phrase 'peace process' was itself considered to be problematic. Speaking in February 1998, before the Good Friday Agreement was

9 Off-the-record interview with authors, 25 February 1998.
10 Ibid.

reached, this observer made the shrewd (if rather pessimistic) point that Northern Ireland was a deeply divided society, it would remain so for the foreseeable future, and that the wounds within the society would take just as long to heal as they had taken to open.

> It depends what you mean by peace. Patently we don't have peace and I think we are a long way from having peace. I don't really think we will ever have peace because we will never have a lack of conflict, we will never have a lack of division. We have had a divided society and it is very clear the lines along which it is divided, in religious terms, in economic terms, and in political and national aspirations. You can work at some of those levels but a lot of those things are never ever going to go away. Those schisms are always going to remain, and as long as they remain we will never have 'peace' so to speak, we are always going to have conflict. So when you ask me what do I think has made a contribution to a peace process, I don't think we have a peace process, or that peace will be the ultimate goal. I would prefer to answer a different question, which is, 'What has advanced the cause of making us a less violent society and a society in which there is a reasonable level of conflict?' It is hard to think of what have been the big events. If I look back over my own lifespan, the big times have been the violent times. The more peaceful times have not been where anything specific has happened. It has been an absence of the big violent times. . . . If I look back over what have been the contributions to peace, it has been a lessening of violence.[11]

When this interviewee was asked why he thought this lessening of violence had taken place – was it, for example, a consequence of P/CRO consciousness-raising or lobbying? – it was suggested (in line with the analysis put forward above) that the move to a less violent society owed more to the changing perspective of those who were directly involved in the conflict, than to the activities of the P/CRO sector which was campaigning against it and trying to deal with its consequences. In this analysis, the 'peace process' had less to do with the arguments of P/CRO organizations, than a realization on the part of the Provisional IRA that their paramilitary campaign was not taking them any closer to their republican objective. Consequently, they decided that a lessening of violence, together with participation in political negotiations with other parties sponsored by the British and Irish governments, would achieve what the 'armed struggle' had

[11] Off-the-record interview with authors, 10 March 1998.

not. This argument proposed that the TUAS strategy of the IRA[12] had resulted in a lessening of violence and a greater degree of 'peace' for broad strategic reasons. The harsh political fact, therefore, was that it was the realities of *war* and the power politics that flowed from it, which had produced a less violent society in Northern Ireland, and not the non-governmental sector or the consciousness-raising activities of the Peace People or the Peace Train.

According to this view, the fact that the dynamics of the conflict had produced the apparently perverse logic that violent acts had made a greater contribution to political progress than the activities of the P/CRO sector, was directly linked to the peripherality of Northern Ireland within the United Kingdom. It was suggested that most of the people living in Great Britain were ambivalent about Northern Ireland and felt little cultural empathy with the region. 'It doesn't matter how many people get killed, or have disastrous lives here or have their lives ruined by a combination of paramilitary violence and the lack of a political process, by and large I think those in Britain don't give a damn, except when it begins to hurt them.'[13] The commitment of the British government to finding a peace agreement in Northern Ireland was seen by this commentator as being a direct consequence of the IRA decision to change the focus of its bombing campaign from Northern Ireland to Britain. The Warrington bombing was mentioned in this context as being an important turning point, as the killing of two young boys by an IRA bomb in 1993 had an emotional resonance for people living in Britain because 'they were ours'. It was pointed out that many similar disasters and tragedies had occurred in Northern Ireland which did not have the same impact as the Warrington bombing due to the fact that people in Britain had become desensitized to such events taking place in a society that they did not see themselves as being part of, or as belonging to.[14] 'I think those sorts of things were major turning

[12] There is some debate as to the precise meaning of the TUAS acronym and whether it refers to Totally Unarmed Strategy, or the Tactical Use of Armed Struggle.

[13] Off-the-record interview with authors, 10 March 1998.

[14] For a more detailed analysis of the socio-political disengagement of Great Britain from Northern Ireland, see Feargal Cochrane, 'Any Takers? The Isolation of Northern Ireland', *Political Studies*, vol. 42, no. 3, Sept. 1994, pp. 378–96.

points. They were violent acts, but they were violent acts that brought the reality of it home to a set of people who had not been committed to making anything happen in peace terms and in political development terms here.'[15] Where the P/CRO sector was credited with making a contribution was at an indirect surface level, and at the emotional level.

> I subscribe to two views of the peace sector. I think it has two roles. It has a sticking-plaster role, it can plaster over the wounds, it can help people to feel a little better when times are bad. But the people whom it affects are people who are not themselves directly political or paramilitary activists, and therefore, because the peace process to me usually does not affect those people, then it has no major impact on the level of violence here. But it does act as an ambulance and as a stretcher and as a Valium tablet when things are going very badly. It definitely has that role and it is quite good at that role, but what impact that has on us in the long term I think is very minimal. But I think that the other role that that sector has, which is just beginning to develop and I think beginning to develop through the likes of the work of the Community Relations Council . . . would be in bedding down political development if you like, to be part of a two-handed strategy, which is on the one hand taking us forward in political terms, so that we do have a framework for agreement, we do have some form of control over our own politics in this country and we do have something that people generally can sign up to on the political side, and hand in hand with that, a community relations set of work which helps to bed that down, which helps to diffuse people's anxieties about it, which helps to explain it, and which helps to avoid what some politicians might do, which would be to reduce any agreement to very simple arguments. I think there is a role there for the NGOs to cut through all of that and make people see the reality of it, and I think they're beginning to develop that. But it is relatively new and we don't know yet how good they might be at it. I think as far as sticking-plasters and being stretcher-bearers go, they've probably been quite good at that . . . but I don't think that has any major impact on the resolution of the conflict.[16]

Several people remarked during the course of this research that the most influential and long-lasting work was done at the micro-level by 'unsung heroes', that is, individuals who worked quietly within their communities. These people were seen as being the glue that had held society together during periods of communal tension and political stalemate. From this perspective, such work, which was based on

15 Off-the-record interview with authors, 10 March 1998.
16 Ibid.

solid foundations and a demonstrable need over a sustained period of time, ultimately had more long-lasting effects in terms of changing attitudes within communities, than work that resulted from high-profile and well-funded community development schemes.

It is certainly true that P/CROs such as the Springfield Inter-Community Development Project would fit into this category of emerging in response to community need and conducting projects that directly benefit the surrounding community with the minimum of publicity. At the same time, however, it would be wrong to adopt a form of inverted snobbery about the P/CRO sector, which assumes that 'small is beautiful', or that such micro-community initiatives are in some sense inevitably more worthy or invested with greater integrity than those that are better resourced or have different social profiles.

To a certain extent it is easy to denigrate the P/CRO sector as being middle-class, 'toffs against terrorism' types, people who shy away from the causes of the conflict and take to the streets with no real sense of strategic objective or political purpose. It is easy to see such activity as simply an emotional response in reaction to 'the latest atrocity', producing a series of unconnected demonstrations and events without any longer-term plan, which loses momentum after the initial emotional reaction has dissipated. However, looked at from a broader perspective, it is possible to argue that the P/CRO sector has provided forums for discussions and dialogue among people, including paramilitary groups, and that these radicals have been sucked into a more sophisticated debate. Sinn Fein politicians, for example, rarely make speeches today that talk about a thirty-two-county socialist republic (apart from at their annual Ard Fheis). While this may remain the political objective, they generally talk more pragmatically today about the 'equality agenda', inclusive engagement with political opponents, and a rights-based approach to political change based upon democracy, human rights and justice. Similarly, few unionists (at least those of a pro-Agreement persuasion) talk anymore about the restoration of majority-rule devolution, but articulate instead a much more inclusive message based on equality of treatment and respect for difference.

Many of those interviewed during the course of this research study pointed to the overlap between the community and political sectors as central to a slow, incremental and positive impact exerted by the

P/CRO community on the political process. From this perspective, the P/CRO sector had encouraged and empowered community activists to come forward and form an extra tier within civil society generally, and the political class in particular. Individuals such as Billy Hutchinson and David Ervine from the Progressive Unionist Party (PUP), who represent radical loyalist opinion, are able at the same time to link these political attitudes into a broader social and economic strategy. It was suggested rather dryly by one well-placed observer, that such people, who did not have a voice in the past, or at least a voice that people took seriously, were now major political actors. 'I think so many people went into the Maze and found God and sought forgiveness, and one or two of them went in and found sociology and politics, and which are the people who have come forward who are useful now? It is not the "God squad" ones!'[17]

While this puts the case rather baldly, it is a reasonable assumption that the growth of such activism, which encouraged people to come forward out of their communities, gave these individuals a new language, a new framework, a new ethic within which they could operate. The P/CRO sector provided the space for such people to grow, and some, such as Billy Hutchinson among many others, have evolved beyond that into the political arena. Consequently, the sector could be said to have played an important role in the peace process in that such individuals within both loyalist and republican communities played a crucial intermediate role between the traditional political process and their communities. Another commentator summed this view up when he claimed that 'There is no way that the old-style politicians could have brokered a deal which would have been sold to those communities [republicans and loyalists], because those communities would not have been part of it if their community leaders had not been part of the talks, and the NGO sector has probably been instrumental in helping that forward'.[18]

This view sees the impact of the P/CRO sector in terms of the production of new social forces that over time have had an important, though *indirect*, bearing on the political process and the level of politically motivated violence in Northern Ireland. This level of impact is seen as being discrete from a direct connection between the

[17] Ibid.
[18] Off-the-record interview with authors, 6 October 1997.

activities of the P/CRO sector and the decisions and policies taken by other actors such as the paramilitaries, the media and the policy-making community. At this level, the effectiveness of the sector is regarded as being peripheral and marginal. While the work of campaigning peace and human rights organizations made known the message that there were a large number of people in Northern Ireland who did not support violence, who wanted a peace settlement, and wished to develop contact between the nationalist and unionist communities, this was a soft, 'touchy-feelie', 'peace-through-hugging' approach, guided by emotions – however well intentioned. In reality, political movement in Northern Ireland was driven by a harder-edged cocktail of competing self-interests and the *realpolitick* assessments of the policy-making community. As one source bluntly expressed it to the authors; 'Things that move things forward are pain!'[19]

It was also remarked that not only was the P/CRO sector ineffective in directly impacting the decision-making process of other actors in the conflict, it could also be seen in negative terms, put at its most pejorative, as being 'worse than useless'. This argument was made specifically about the large-scale movements such as the Peace People and others, who tried to mobilize mass opinion through public demonstrations, marches and vigils. It was claimed that to some degree this activity had given 'peace' a bad name, as the anti-violence protest had become politicized and easily denigrated as the peddling of soft and trite messages by a self-appointed middle-class élite. These movements, which engaged in 'grand gestures', were contrasted unfavourably by many observers, with those that worked quietly on the ground to address a set of much more focused objectives that gained credibility, not through moral crusading, but by demonstrating their practical benefits to the communities they were working within.

> If you look at people like Billy Robinson in Counteract . . . what the Billy Robinsons' and the Mari FitzDuffs' and the Will Glendinnings' of this world have been doing [the former and current directors of the Community Relations Council respectively], is convincing people by their actions, and by making things work at local levels. By solving problems they are showing people who are really up against it, that

[19] Off-the-record interview with authors, 10 March 1998.

> resolution can take place if you work at it and you act according to a certain set of rules. It's like so many of those things that happen nowadays, that you have a lot of people who have had a valuable experience there in resolving some kind of local conflict, who now do believe that that kind of peaceful resolution process can take place, and I think almost by osmosis, those people have then made their voices heard within their communities, and that has become something that politicians and community activists have latched onto as a way of making things work. So, quietly and behind the scenes, and working at a local level, I think that whole movement has had much greater impact than the grand Peace Train, Peace People, and so forth.[20]

Mirror mirror on the wall, who is the fairest P/CRO of all?

For those P/CROs who try to change public opinion, or at least alert it to issues relating to the conflict, the ability to gain access to the media might reasonably be taken as a measure of their impact. Of course, not all of these groups actively seek media attention and some, such as Quaker House, regard it as an obstacle to the effective development of their work. However, the relationship between the media and P/CRO sector is an important indicator of public visibility and, therefore, impact upon public attitudes.

One source saw the relationship between the P/CRO groups and the media not in terms of a group of idealists being squeezed through a filter of political cynicism, but rather viewed the sector as being a victim of the short-term attention spans of the medium. It was suggested that both the print and broadcast media had a need to reduce complex issues into simple messages, in a way similar to that in which politicians were forced to communicate. As a consequence, the media has often contributed to an image of Northern Ireland as being a hugely divided society; in reality, however, there are many levels at which it is not divided at all. Thus, while the P/CRO sector was generally thought to have received about the right amount of coverage, it was believed that the media had distorted the picture by conveying very black-and-white messages, which in turn had resulted in a negative contribution to peace. The media has been so intent on mapping the fractures in community relations, the divisions within society and the sectarianism and violence that this produces, it has failed to produce a balanced picture. 'What I think

20 Ibid.

we've done is we've put a big tyre lever in what was a small gap, and we've levered it very open, and what we have failed to do, the media, people like me and politicians, is to look for the strata at which we make connections, and to try to promote that in some way. It has been our careers if you like, not to promote division, but to talk about it and highlight it and measure it.'[21]

It was not suggested in any of our discussions that the media had under-represented the P/CRO sector as a whole, though the point was made repeatedly to the authors that journalists had their own agendas, which often skewed the message that many organizations were trying to convey. One observer made the point that the media were overly cynical and made it difficult for many organizations to convey a positive story without being portrayed as politically naive:

> I think actually the media have been incredibly destructive in the conflict in Northern Ireland. . . . Not necessarily – though sometimes – the local media, but certainly the 'national' UK media have always talked down any efforts towards peace, in that they have tried to pour cold water [over positive developments] and have been more impressed by what made a good story, than actually the outcome on the ground.[22]

Another interviewee drew on personal experience when making a similar point, namely that the perceived 'news value' was often tangential to the agenda of the particular organization. It was emphasized by this source and others, that coverage of P/CROs by the media was patchy and often owed more to the relative 'sexiness' of the issue and whether it was photogenic, than to any of its intrinsic merits.

> I'm not at all positive in broad terms about the role of media. Until recently, I think, the media has always tried to simplify and fascinate and therefore the more photogenic opportunities have got [greater attention]. Certainly the media has always been into having balanced conversations, but that often means it doesn't go anywhere! In my own experience, for example, one of my friends was Sean Armstrong, who was the first youth worker shot. When we opened a playground in his memory, we couldn't get any press publicity, because it was an awkward time, they had a long way to travel and it was not a high-profile story. Now I think actually that trying to create a children's play area in memory of a youth worker who had been shot . . . that was a story that should be told. I spent four years on the BBC council here [and] I just felt

21 Ibid.
22 Off-the-record interview with authors, 25 February 1998.

> that their whole approach to covering that educative and community-building social policy [area has been lacking] and that media and the broadsheets have not, in the main, critically engaged with the subtleties and complexities of [the issues]. Now, of course, the other side is, maybe the organizations should have simplified their work a bit more so they would be more amenable to the media, but with some of these things you can't. . . . So I do think the media have not looked at their [strategic purpose]; they have insisted on this tradition [whereby] they 'have to report the news', but I think actually they have shaped the news and diminished certain possibilities.[23]

Due partly to the relatively small size of Northern Ireland, relationships between the local media and the leading personnel of many P/CROs are familiar. The existence of a reasonably well-developed social network has obviously increased the access of P/CROs to the media, so public demonstrations or other photogenic events are usually covered on the pretext of being a good 'news' story or as being in 'the public interest'. Rarely does the media ask more complex questions at such times, as to, for instance, what *impact* the demonstration will have on public opinion in the longer term, or how it fits into the strategic objective of those organizing it.

It would be fair to say that despite the media attention the P/CRO sector has managed to generate, there is a negative perception within many areas of Northern Ireland of what is often referred to in pejorative terms as the 'community relations industry'. This is partly based on class divisions, particularly the fact that the middle class, which predominantly populates the 'community relations industry', is seen by many people in working-class urban areas as being remote from their lives and the issues which concern their area. Organizations such as the Community Relations Council and the Cultural Traditions Group are sometimes derided as being 'toffs against terrorism', outsiders who seek to deliver peace and harmony to communities they do not understand or live amongst. There was a consensus among those interviewed for this book (several of whom could be described as being part of the community relations industry) that a stigmatization had occurred and that potentially valuable work was being undervalued because of the general image problem which the sector has, namely, of being populated by a middle-class community who had failed to impact within interface areas of Northern Ireland.

[23] Off-the-record interview with authors, 26 February 1998.

Conflicting strategies

As discussed earlier in this study, there are essentially three strategic approaches that the P/CRO sector takes in relation to reconciliation and conflict resolution activity. One is cross-community work, where Catholics and Protestants are brought together to participate jointly in events and dialogue. A second approach is inter-community work, where an organization will work within and between two communities to address common problems without necessarily maximizing contact between opposing groups. The third (and most controversial) strategy is single-identity work. These groups focus upon one community and seek primarily to redress social and economic deprivation as a precursor to engaging in contact with members from the 'other' community. All of these approaches have advantages and drawbacks. However, we were particularly interested in looking at the relationship between cross-community work and single-identity activity. It has been argued by single-identity organizations within Northern Ireland that cross-community work was an ephemeral exercise, conducted primarily by middle-class philanthropists who did not fully understand the issues in sectarian conflict or the practical realities faced within interface areas. Proponents of cross-community activity, on the other hand, often see single-identity advocates as evading the challenges posed by anti-sectarian work and simply accentuating differences (at worst, wallowing in them) rather than helping to resolve or lessen communal tensions.

Many of the people interviewed during the research for this book accepted that there were problems with both approaches and that neither cross-community nor single-identity work has dealt adequately with the growing levels of sectarian polarization in Northern Ireland. When it was suggested to one observer that single-identity work was, in theory, a more secure approach than cross-community activity in that it was insulated from a deterioration in the macro-political environment, which often destroyed initiatives designed to bring 'the two communities' together, the point was made very strongly that single-identity work was doing little to assist reconciliation or decrease community conflict. This source believed that single-identity groups were, for the most part, engaged in a resource-acquisition exercise facilitated by the funding criteria, and had no real desire to address or break down sectarian conflict. It was claimed, for example, that the Peace and Reconciliation money granted by the European Union after the ceasefires of 1994, contained no overt requirement for reconciliation objectives to be built in to funding applications. Consequently, because reconciliation criteria were not tied in to these grants, the EU money simply became another set of funds for community groups to capture.

> I think that the talk of single-identity work is a complete self-delusion, frankly. I don't actually see why it helps Protestants to talk to Catholics, that they are more confident about themselves. The problem that we have isn't that people aren't able to talk to each other in their own community and lack the confidence to do so. The problem is that they live in communities that are hermetically sealed from others and they don't talk to the other side. I've never understood the logic in saying that the way to learn about the other side is to talk to yourself![24]

It was suggested to this critic that the logic comes from the sense of fear and insecurity within both communities and from the myths that have been built up on both sides about the 'other' community. Thus, if resources were channelled into some of these deprived urban areas, such myths and beliefs might lessen and make people more amenable to engaging positively with those whom they currently regard as their enemies and actual or potential oppressors. The critic of the single-identity approach quoted above remained unconvinced by this argument:

> This is just a kind of vulgar Marxism. That sense of economic determinism is crazy. I will just look at it from my own point of view. What was it that made me rethink? At that point in life it was the challenges of the civil rights movement. . . . The fact is that the civil rights movement, which was a direct challenge from the Catholic community, made me rethink what I was about, and I don't see how I could have ever got to that point no matter how many days and nights I'd spent in the local unionist hall or Orange hall talking to people of broadly similar minds. . . . I just think that it is striking that the advocates of single-identity work are strikingly single-identity [in nature]![25]

This rather damning view of the single-identity approach was put to another informed observer of the P/CRO sector in Northern Ireland. He was asked whether he accepted the argument put forward by single-identity organizations, that before people living in deprived interface areas could realistically engage in meaningful cross-community

[24] Off-the-record interview with authors, 10 March 1998.
[25] Ibid.

work, it was necessary first to build the capacity within their community, in order that people had the self-confidence to engage with those from the 'outside'?

> I don't buy [that argument] at all. I buy it in theory . . . because theoretically you could say, yes, you must have communities out there who are just unsure about themselves and who don't have the infrastructure within their communities in order to move forward and to engage with the other community. But I think that is a middle-class analysis. My experience of looking at single-identity groups was that that was never the case and there are some hideous stories about so-called single-identity community relations groups, where I am quite sure that it is not confidence in their own identity that's happening, but it is countenancing your identity to the extent that you are actually creating a deeper level of division. I have hard evidence from some of those groups that the last thing they want is to engage with the other community.[26]

Once again the assessment of the single-identity model is that it tends to reinforce ethnic identity, fuel a victim-culture, and corral communities behind their tribal fences, rather than diminish stereotypes or increase inter-communal understanding and toleration. It was suggested that while there remains a place for single- identity work to make a contribution, a more strategic criteria-led approach needed to be developed to fund the worthwhile P/CROs and weed out those that were purely interested in resource acquisition. In practical terms this will be a difficult task, as a strong sense of victimhood exists within many single-identity groups and any re-evaluation by funders, or strategic re-targeting of resources away from such P/CROs, will almost inevitably be seen by those organizations as discriminatory and political. Nevertheless, it seems clear that this nettle will have to be grasped in order to separate the worthwhile single-identity P/CROs that are serious about their conflict resolution goals, from those semi-professional 'whingers' who are more interested in milking cash cows and in building up communal differences than breaking them down.

While this could be seen as a rather damning assessment of single-identity P/CROs, there is also a more positive story to tell. The point was made several times by commentators during the research for this book, that in some circumstances, and within certain contexts, single-identity work was the only realistic peace/conflict resolution strategy

[26] Off-the-record interview with authors, 10 March 1998.

available. While many were aware of the inadequacies exhibited by some single-identity groups, there was a reluctance to condemn such organizations en masse. There was a recognition that groups engaged in single-identity initiatives had to bring their communities with them and demonstrate the practical benefits of their work. If they failed to do so, they would lose influence within their constituencies and consequently their leadership roles. 'I actually think there is a lot more work that can be done around the single-identity approach, because very often what is called single-identity work, is actually functional work in a local community, [e.g.] to get a playground. The actual single identity in terms of the "identity" work, is very often not done, but where it is done . . . it can be extremely important.'[27]

While opinion is clearly divided on its impact, it is obvious that single-identity work tends to occur within communities with a strongly defined sense of identity and that this identity is encouraged and reinforced through capacity-building, rather than made more amenable to cross-community interaction. Depending on one's outlook, this can either engender community confidence and provide empowerment, or, less positively, act to accentuate and promote communal differences. As one observer remarked wryly, 'there is certain evidence to suggest that it can be used as an excuse to prepare people for the *fight*, rather than to prepare people for the *meeting*'.[28] It is clear that while single-identity work has its positive aspects, it can very easily be used as a means to buttress particular political and religious ideologies that are exclusivist, supremacist and judgemental, rather than pluralist. Good single-identity work was generally seen as being that which attempted to introduce people to the 'other', or at least acknowledge them, if it was impossible in practical terms to facilitate interaction between communities. However, it was pointed out to the authors repeatedly that there were many bad examples of single-identity work where this was not an objective, and where a scapegoating and blame culture had developed towards the 'other' community.

While single identity P/CRO activity clearly has its critics, cross-community work is not without its difficulties either. To some degree, cross-community P/CROs are more vulnerable than their single-

[27] Off-the-record interview with authors, 25 February 1998.
[28] Off-the-record interview with authors, 26 February 1998.

identity cousins, as they are effectively at the mercy of the wider macro-political environment within which such initiatives try to operate. Those who participated in the research were asked to address the criticism that cross-community work was, in the final analysis, ineffective, as several months' work could be wiped out by a single sectarian riot or act of politically motivated violence. It was argued in response that this was an occupational hazard for such organizations and that it was not realistic for them to wait until the macro-political environment became more conducive to their message, as this would be impractical and would also lead to a reactive and overly conservative culture within P/CROs.

It was pointed out by several commentators that the way to combat the fragility of this cross-community activity was to lobby organizations at the centre of society, in the public and private sectors, to 'mainstream' anti-sectarianism as an issue. Not as a matter of civic responsibility or social altruism, but as an issue of management, and an issue of good business and self-interest. In this scheme, models of dealing with difficulties around sectarianism would be integrated into the day-to-day work fabric and 'mainstreamed', rather than regarded as add-ons or optional extras to make the mission statement sound more responsible or politically correct. There was a consensus among the people interviewed that integrating a community relations strategy into all departments of government and across all sectors was the most sensible strategic approach to develop as this would facilitate a fire prevention rather than a firefighting role.

While there is clearly a role for the statutory agencies in helping these organizations to become more effective in peace and conflict resolution work, it would also be fair to say that the P/CRO sector itself shares some responsibility for its own shortcomings and cannot simply blame funders, policy-makers or the media for the difficulties it faces. There is a need for these organizations to think in a much more co-ordinated, holistic and strategic way about what they are trying to achieve. One well-placed observer of the voluntary sector interviewed put it like this: 'You never get a real sense that those people who are working in peace and reconciliation and human rights have any coherent overall presence. There is very little co-ordination, there is very little apparent exchange of practice and ideas, and there is very little of a sense of an overall evolving NGO-type agenda.'[29] The same source pointed out on a more optimistic note that there were encouraging signs from within the sector that a number of NGOs that did not traditionally view their role as being within the P/CR field, such as the Confederation of British Industries (CBI), the Irish Congress of Trade Unions (ICTU) and the Northern Ireland Council for Voluntary Action (NICVA), were much more upfront today about their relationship to the political conflict than they had been in the past, and were becoming increasingly prepared to adopt a small-'p' political role. This was clearly demonstrated following the Good Friday Agreement as these organizations positioned themselves on the pro-Agreement side and publicly supported a 'Yes' vote in the subsequent referendum.

The 'So what?' question

For the last thirty years of politically motivated conflict in Northern Ireland, P/CROs have tirelessly mined the seam of hope within an atmosphere of increasing polarization and sectarianism. Countless people have joined such organizations and have given generously of their time and energy, often for little material reward, while some have paid for such involvement with their lives and more have suffered intimidation and harassment. Hundreds of millions of pounds have been poured into this sector over the period by successive British governments and lately by the European Union, to fund a plethora of community reconciliation and community development projects. It seems reasonable, therefore, to ask whether all of this activity and effort has had any effect on the nature of the conflict and the society within which that conflict takes place?

During the last six years, Northern Ireland has experienced a peace process, which, on 10 April 1998, culminated in a historic political agreement between unionists and nationalists. The hard question to ask is, did the activity of the P/CRO sector influence the development of this political/peace process and, if so, in what ways? Alternatively, would this chain of events have occurred anyway, regardless of the work that these organizations have carried out over the last thirty years?

It is clear that the impact of the P/CRO sector on political progress

[29] Off-the-record interview with authors, 10 March 1998.

has been indirect rather than direct, gradual rather than dramatic. It is impossible in the context of Northern Ireland to point to a specific political event or a specific P/CRO and claim that it marked a turning point in the impact of this sector on the peace process. The role of such organizations has been osmosis-like, and almost imperceptible in its effect. A suitable metaphor might be that of watching the tide coming in. At any one snapshot in time, it is very difficult to determine whether it is coming in or going out as the waves ebb and flow. However, after several hours, when you find that the water is up around your knees, a conclusion is easier to reach.

While it is difficult to point to a concrete cause and effect with regard to the P/CRO sector and the peace process in Northern Ireland, and although its impact on the political process has been peripheral rather than central, it would be reasonable to conclude that Northern Ireland would have been a lot worse off without its contribution to peace and conflict resolution over the last thirty years. This sector filled a vacuum left by the political actors in the 1970s and 1980s, and created a visible tier of people who presented some alternative to the political nihilism exhibited within the constitutional debate for most of the period from 1969 until the early 1990s. While the P/CRO sector may not have had a dramatic perceivable impact on the course of the conflict, it was often the glue that held society together during the worst days of the 'troubles'. Had this 'stretcher-bearer' role not existed over the last thirty years, the social impact of the political conflict on people living within Northern Ireland would have been much greater. Paul Nolan, formerly Director of the Workers' Educational Association, has reflected on the role of the voluntary and community sector during the conflict, and concludes that from the earliest stages of violence in 1970, individual, autonomous and unorganized initiatives were taking place:

> All over Northern Ireland there were people trying to help the families that had been burnt out, or establishing food co-operatives, or taking kids from the frontline areas off on holiday, or setting up peoples' assemblies, or trying to get dialogue between Protestants and Catholics. Or whatever. There was prodigious energy, and an optimism that this ragbag of people could create a sort of counter-culture . . . that would not only challenge the rising sectarianism, but would give expression to a new radical politics.
>
> . . . Throughout thirty years of communal conflict the network of local community organizations provided a kind of invisible stitching

> which held the fabric of this society together. When, as sometimes happens, this argument is pitched too high or when – another occasional failing – local voluntary chieftains are seen to be taking too much credit onto themselves for the success of the peace process, then an understandable resentment is provoked.[30]

While the individual impacts of these groups were small, often nebulous, and negative as well as positive, these organizations provided a continuity and 'normality' within the region, which demonstrated to the outside world that a substantial body of opinion existed which wanted the conflict to be resolved.

On a more practical level, the concentration of many P/CROs on processes rather than outcomes, led many to develop the intellectual debate on issues such as human rights, equality and social inclusion, and to scrutinize government legislation around these issues. Christopher McCrudden has written about the role that such groups have played in the debate over equality issues, particularly with regard to the last Conservative government's introduction of Policy Appraisal and Fair Treatment (PAFT) guidelines in 1994:

> PAFT was an attempt to establish a procedure within Government decision making by which the principles of equity and equality could be made effective. . . . In a sustained attempt to encourage groups to use the guidelines, the Committee on the Administration of Justice (CAJ), a Northern Ireland human rights NGO, organised briefing sessions on the guidelines for a range of interested voluntary and community organizations. The NGOs responded with enthusiasm. A loose coalition was born that was dedicated to putting PAFT into effect.[31]

While PAFT's practical impact on equality issues in Northern Ireland may be contested, this provides a useful example of the way in which P/CROs have made an important contribution to the political debate within Northern Ireland.

The impact of P/CROs in comparative perspective

An assessment of P/CRO activity in Northern Ireland may be helped by looking at the P/CRO role within other divided societies such as South Africa and Israel/Palestine. It would be reasonable to conclude

[30] Paul Nolan, *Fortnight*, September 2000, pp. 28–29.

[31] Christopher McCrudden, 'Equality and the Good Friday Agreement', in J. Ruane and J. Todd (eds.), *After the Good Friday Agreement: Analysing Political*

that, while the context varied within these different regions, P/CROs were all active in playing at least an indirect role in the political processes that led to peace agreements in the 1990s.

The impact of South African P/CROs can be seen at a number of levels. It may be said that the P/CROs, taken as a movement, had a major effect on the peace process in South Africa. 'How would I characterise their role? They weren't principal players as it were, they didn't have a decisive role, but they had an extremely significant role.'[32] Rupert Taylor et al. (1998) have identified several categories within which the South African groups impacted on the political process, that ultimately led to the ending of the apartheid system. Firstly, they promoted an alternative identity to that of race. Apartheid was based on the concept of separate racial identities. However, the South African P/CROs worked to promote the concept of a non-racial South Africa and move away from the white/black division that defined the old order. Their alternative (which is now accepted by most people and underpins the new system) was a South African citizenship based on a shared national identity.[33]

Secondly, the South African P/CROs built relationships between the black and white communities, which had previously been not only separate, but extremely suspicious of and antagonistic towards one another. This was an important component of presenting a non-threatening future for the white population, where change would not be about blacks taking over from and dominating the white community, but about moving into a new politics based on partnership.[34] Thirdly, at the more practical level, the P/CRO sector had material resources, intellectual skills and vast international networks which the anti-apartheid political movement was able to tap into and use

Change in Northern Ireland (University College Dublin Press, 1999), pp. 100–1).

32 Albie Sachs, quoted in the Final Report of the South African ISPO team. R. Taylor, A. Egan, A. Habib, J. Cock, A. Lekwane and M. Shaw (unpublished report, South Africa, 1998)

33 R. Taylor, A. Egan, A. Habib, J. Cock, A. Lekwane and M. Shaw, 'Executive Summary: International Study of Peace and Conflict Resolution Organizations – South Africa'. Unpublished paper presented to the Third Conference of the International Society for Third Sector Research, Geneva, 8–12 July 1998.

34 Ibid.

very effectively.[35] Fourthly, many P/CROs were very effective at producing research that showed the human and material costs of the apartheid system. This was based on logic rather than morality or ideology, the central message being that apartheid, even in its own terms, was an inefficient and failed policy.[36]

The picture is more depressing within Israel/Palestine with regard to the impact of P/CROs on the 'peace process', than is the case in either South Africa or Northern Ireland. While there has been a political agreement (of sorts) between the élites, represented by the Oslo and Wye River agreements, the relationships between the conflict parties have not been substantially transformed, despite the best efforts of peace groups. In fact, if anything, they have got worse, as extremists and 'spoilers' on both sides have reacted violently to the peace agreements, increasing mistrust and antagonism between the communities. However, while Israelis and Palestinians may not have transformed their relationship with one another, the peace movement has nevertheless had an important impact upon the political process. At the very least, it has changed the way in which both sides view their self-interest. In the past it was a 'zero sum' equation, in that any perceived gain for the Israelis was a perceived loss for the Palestinians and vice versa. The Israeli peace movement seems successfully to have influenced Israeli public opinion (and the political actors) towards the view that something approaching a 'positive sum' equation can be reached through the formula of land for peace.

The picture within the Palestinian community is the most bleak. If the Palestinian P/CROs have had any impact, it is at the level of providing support to their beleaguered communities rather than in transforming conflict relations between Arabs and Israelis or influencing the peace process at a political level.

> One can hardly begin to talk of the effect of 'Peace and Conflict Resolution Organizations and their role in Peace Building' when for the most part, there are no peace and conflict resolution organizations in Palestine, there is very little peace building being done, and there is even less peace building in the larger context that such activity could be considered a part of. In a sense then, one should not blind oneself by

[35] Ibid.
[36] Ibid.

illusions of an imminent Palestinian/Israeli or Arab/Israeli peace initiative, when such initiatives are virtually paralyzed.[37]

In Northern Ireland the impact of the P/CRO sector on the political process and social fabric of the region is more obvious than in Israel/Palestine, though perhaps less direct than was the case in South Africa.

The point was made on several occasions to the authors during the research, that one of the reasons why the political conflict in Northern Ireland did not escalate to the level of violence witnessed in places like Bosnia, was because there was some acceptance within public opinion of basic democratic norms and a fundamental notion of human rights. There *has* been a failure on the part of the NGO sector generally within Northern Ireland to capitalize on this basic consensus and develop it, due to their inability to construct a persuasive political language that goes beyond saying 'violence is bad and dialogue is good'. There has also been some difficulty in developing strategic objectives, fuelled by jealousies, rivalries and tensions within and between P/CROs themselves.

Notwithstanding these drawbacks, the sector as a whole has succeeded in moving the political process in a positive direction and stimulating creative thinking, without necessarily being given credit for having done so. It was suggested by several observers that had the work of the P/CRO organizations not taken place over the last thirty years there would have been little debate or understanding about the basic values and principles of a settlement. While arguments surrounding institutions may have gone on between the politicians, and the merits or otherwise of a devolved assembly in Northern Ireland and North–South bodies would have been discussed, there would have been little *philosophical* discussion to breathe life into such concepts. 'What the NGO sector has been able to do is to stand back a bit and try and articulate what the values should be of a deal, and that has been crucial, and I think we do now have the basic language to put the architecture together.'[38]

[37] Professor Manuel Hassassian, Bethlehem University, leader of the Palestinian team, ISPO, paper presented at the Third Conference of the International Society for Third Sector Research (ISTR), Geneva, 8–12 July 1998.

[38] Off-the-record interview with authors, 10 March 1998.

Conclusion

It is clear from this chapter that a range of opinion exists as to whether peace and conflict resolution organizations have made an effective contribution to the political process in Northern Ireland, and more specifically, to the development of the peace process. Views range from a positive notion that they developed a new vocabulary and public consciousness around a peace agenda, to the more critical assertion that they failed to get beyond a very superficial level that may have gained short-term publicity but left little lasting impression on society.

We take the view that the answer to the question as to whether the P/CRO sector has had an effective impact upon the peace process, depends a great deal on how that question is framed. At the micro-level, in terms of a specific correlation between the actions of individual groups and the course of the political conflict, it has to be said that there is little evidence to suggest that P/CROs have had a significant influence on events. A much more convincing case could be made that their activities were peripheral to the search for a political settlement in Northern Ireland. Nevertheless, the small-scale activities and quiet work of these organizations, while insignificant at the individual level, can be seen to have had a major impact on civil society in Northern Ireland when looked at cumulatively. It is at the macro-level, when we look at the *sector* rather than the groups within it, where the greatest impact can be found. There are a number of areas that should be highlighted. The first is that the unspectacular 'drip-in-the-bucket' work conducted by the sector provided avenues of contact for political actors who were not able to interact at the public level. While this dialogue and debate had little tangible impact on the level of violence at the time, it assisted the process of political education and re-evaluation, which ultimately contributed to the republican and loyalist ceasefires in the autumn of 1994.

Secondly, while there appear to be few champions remaining of the large-scale peace organizations that placed an emphasis on high-level public campaigns to mobilize opposition to violence, a lot of support exists for the low-level work carried out by individuals and small organizations away from the glare of publicity. The overt campaigns designed to mobilize public support were well motivated but ultimately ephemeral in their effects. Whether because they misunderstood the causes of the conflict, or due to personality clashes and organizational implosion, these movements could not sustain themselves and too often became emotional gestures (valid in themselves) rather than providing rational alternatives to the conflict. The provision of an emotional outlet rather than a coherent process out of the conflict, resulted in diminishing returns for those involved, as people became tired of attending public demonstrations and rallies that had no appreciable effect on the level of paramilitary violence.

A comparison between the well-meaning but perhaps muddle-headed approach of the highly visible large-scale P/CROs that concentrated on public consciousness-raising, and low-level community-based anti-sectarian initiatives, results in a more favourable outcome for the latter. The value of such groups can be seen in their positive practical effects on specific communities. In place of the high moral rhetoric of the peace movements, this work provided something tangible for people to work with, and was consequently more long lasting and valuable than strategies that involved public protest.

Thirdly, most of those interviewed during the course of this research believed that the situation would have been much worse had it not been for the work of the P/CRO sector over the last thirty years. As well as playing a 'stretcher-bearer' role and acting as a comfort for the worst aspects of the conflict, these groups, for all their inadequacies, provided evidence of the desire for peace in Northern Ireland.

Finally, at least four of the political parties involved in negotiating the Good Friday Agreement have been substantially influenced by community sector politics, and many of these people have been elected to the Northern Ireland Assembly to implement the Agreement. Perhaps the most obvious of these is the Northern Ireland Women's Coalition (NIWC), whose members have been substantially drawn from the NGO sector. While the Women's Coalition has struggled to obtain significant electoral support, it has attempted to infuse the political process with the NGO values of inclusiveness, dialogue and tolerance. It has to be admitted, of course, that many within the political process in Northern Ireland remain immune to the charms of such ideas. Nevertheless, there is tangible evidence that the ideas and ethos promoted by the NGO sector have impacted directly on the political structures of Northern Ireland.

The Civic Forum[39] is an aspect of the Good Friday Agreement that is often forgotten in the publicity that accompanies high-profile issues such as new cross-border bodies, prisoner releases and weapons decommissioning, yet this is an integral part of the Agreement and one that was actively promoted by the Women's Coalition and the P/CRO sector generally. The forum is a revolutionary idea in terms of Northern Ireland politics as it is a non-party-political structure that gives institutional recognition to the other stake-holders in civil society and is envisaged as acting as a resource for the explicitly political lower chamber. It is too early to assess the impact that the Civic Forum will have on the political process in Northern Ireland. There will inevitably be some uneasy shuffling of feet at Stormont, as politicians and representatives from the voluntary and community sector try to avoid stepping on one another's corns. It is quite likely that friction will be generated and animosity created as these unusual partners in government begin to work together, before a positive equilibrium is established. *Fortnight* magazine makes the point sardonically:

> The political mathematics of the Forum are, like Eamon de Valera, a riddle wrapped around an enigma. Business and the Trade Unions get fifteen seats. Farmers get two. The Voluntary Sector get a whopping eighteen. Looked at in cold economic clout, this is madness. . . . Community Groups can justly argue that the social 'added value' of their work adds up to far more than the economic worth of their annual turnover. However, the calculation which privileges NICVA or the NIVT over the CBI or ICTU is based upon concession politics masquerading as the politics of compassion. It is also a very useful way of corralling and controlling the loud voices of the voluntary sector. Party politicians in an unguarded moment will happily share the loathing they feel for the 'busybodies' of the voluntary sector. . . . The notion that 'civil society' is a stabilising force in a divided society stems largely from the events of a

[39] The Good Friday Agreement set out the terms for this institution in the following way: 'A Consultative Civic Forum will be established. It will comprise representatives of the business, trade union and voluntary sectors, and other such sectors as agreed by the First Minister and the Deputy First Minister. It will act as a consultative mechanism on social, economic and cultural issues.' *The Agreement*, paragraph 34 (Belfast: HMSO, April 1998), p. 9, in F. Cochrane, 'Beyond the Political Elites: A Comparative Analysis of the Roles and Impacts of Community-Based NGOs in Conflict Resolution Activity', *Civil Wars*, vol. 3, no. 2, Summer 2000, p. 19.

> decade ago in eastern and central Europe, in particular the Velvet Revolution and the public opposition of the Civic Forum. The sight of charismatic dramatists and poets peacefully dismantling Stalinism acted as a consolation prize to western lefties who could no longer bear to use the word 'socialism'. . . . If the idea of civil society is limited to high mindedness, rather than grubby reality, it becomes, as Rieff notes, 'a theological notion, not a political or sociological one'.[40]

While we shall have to wait and see whether the Civic Forum makes a worthwhile contribution to the political process in Northern Ireland, it seems fair to conclude at this point that this novel institution would not have been created without the intellectual contribution made by the P/CRO sector over the duration of the conflict. More fundamentally perhaps, it would be fair to conclude that 'civil society' in Northern Ireland is relatively healthy, certainly in comparison to other sites of recent ethnic conflict such as Israel/Palestine, Bosnia or Kosovo. Individuals, P/CROs and other networks such as the churches, trade unions, business groups and the media, have largely bought into the philosophical ethos promoted by peace/conflict resolution organizations over the last thirty years. These groups are populated by a sophisticated, politically literate and highly networked community, capable of mobilizing and leading their constituencies. This was perfectly illustrated during the referendum campaign following the Good Friday Agreement. At very short notice, an independent 'Yes' campaign emerged, largely drawn from the voluntary sector, in support of the political agreement. This reflected many of the features of P/CROs detailed earlier in this study, namely, charismatic and dynamic leadership, a sense of civic responsibility, and an optimism that their efforts could 'make a difference'. One of its founders recollected the motivations for starting the campaign and the positive impact this eventually had on some of those who had negotiated the political settlement:

> On St Patrick's Day (17 March) 1998, a group of people met privately in Belfast to discuss the peace process and what would happen if the ongoing Talks resulted in an agreement by Easter, as had been promised. . . . The outcome of the lunchtime discussion . . . was that a positive campaign would be needed to mobilise a sceptical citizenry that a deal had, indeed, been done and was worthy of support. . . . But who were we – other than a group of friends and colleagues, some drawn

[40] Leader, 'Uncivil Society' in *Fortnight*, July 2000, p. 5.

> from the voluntary sector and others from the business sector – and what was our legitimacy? We knew we had none, in electoral terms, but we felt we had rights as citizens and as inhabitants of Northern Ireland – and, indeed, a duty to help the political process along.
>
> . . . The Ulster Unionist Party had begun the Campaign with a reserved, even cold, attitude towards us. They felt we might be too avant-garde, even exotic, for their constituency and they seemed to distrust our motives. They had done the deal, they knew their own constituency, they would sell the deal and they would win the political fruits – went their argument. One senior figure was reported to have suggested that 'when this Campaign is over, these people should be cleaning the streets, where they belong'. But all that was to change. By the end of the Campaign, we were making daily visits to the UUP's Headquarters at Glengall Street, debating strategy and tactics, helping with postering, briefing on media appearances and advising and supporting advertising.[41]

It may be concluded that the independent 'Yes' campaign was the result of a healthy civil society, and that the eventual vote of 71 per cent in favour of the Good Friday Agreement in the May 1998 referendum would have been significantly lower had it not been for its contribution to the political process.

Only time will tell whether the Good Friday Agreement will ultimately survive and whether unionists and nationalists will be able to continue the difficult task of building peace within a deeply divided society. However, while obstacles remain, the efforts to do this will be significantly advanced by the activity and commitment of the P/CRO sector within Northern Ireland.

41 Quintin Oliver, *Working for 'Yes': The Story of the May 1998 Referendum in Northern Ireland* (The 'Yes' Campaign, Belfast: 1998), p. 9 and pp. 79–81.

Select Bibliography

Abbas, M., *Through Secret Channels*. Reading: Garnet Publishing, 1995.

Acheson, N. and A. Williamson, *Voluntary Action and Social Policy in Northern Ireland*, Aldershot: Avebury, 1995.

Allison, L., 'Sport and Civil Society', *Political Studies*, vol. 46, no. 4, Sept. 1998.

Arthur, P., *Government and Politics of Northern Ireland*, London: Longman, 1987.

Arthur, P. and K. Jeffery, *Northern Ireland since 1968*. Oxford: Blackwell, 1988.

Bardon, J., *A History of Ulster*. Belfast: Blackstaff Press, 1992.

Bloomfield, K., *Stormont in Crisis*. Belfast, Blackstaff Press, 1994.

Bew, P. and G. Gillespie, *Northern Ireland: A Chronology of the Troubles 1968–1993*. Dublin: Gill and Macmillan, 1993.

Brown, M. E., (ed.) *The International Dimensions of Internal Conflict*, Massachusets, MIT Press, 1996.

Buckland, P., *James Craig*. Dublin: Gill and Macmillan, 1980.

Carnegie Commission on Preventing Deadly Conflict; *Preventing Deadly Conflict: Final Report with Executive Summary*, Washington: Carnegie Commission on Preventing Deadly Conflict, 1997.

Clarke, G., 'Non-Governmental Organizations (NGOs) and Politics in the Developing World' *Political Studies*, vol. 46, no. 1, March 1998.

Cochrane, F., *Unionist Politics and the Politics of Unionism since the Anglo-Irish Agreement*, Cork University Press, 1997.

Cochrane, F., 'Beyond the Political Elites: A Comparative Analysis of the Roles and Impacts of Community-Based NGOs in Conflict Resolution Activity.' *Civil Wars*, Vol. 3, No. 2, Summer 2000, pp. 1–22.

Cochrane, F., 'The Past in the Present', in P. Mitchell and R. Wilford (eds.) *Politics in Northern Ireland*. Oxford: Westview Press, 1999.

Cochrane. F. 'Any Takers? The Isolation of Northern Ireland'. *Political Studies*, vol. 42, no. 3, Sept. 1994. pp. 378–96.

Corbin, J., *Gaza First: The Secret Norway Channel To Peace Between Israel and the PLO*. London: Bloomsbury, 1994.

Cox, M., A. Guelke, & F. Stephen, (eds) *A Farewell To Arms? From 'Long War' to 'Long Peace' in Northern Ireland*. Manchester: Manchester University Press, 2000.

Darby, J., *Northern Ireland: Background to the Conflict*, Belfast: Appletree Press, 1983.

Darby, J., *Scorpions in A Bottle*, London: Minority Rights Association, 1997.
Democratic Dialogue, *New Order? International Models of Peace and Reconciliation*. Belfast, Democratic Dialogue, Report no. 9, May 1998.
Dunn, S., ed., *Facets of the Conflict in Northern Ireland*, London: Macmillan, 1995.
Fraser, G., and V., Morgan, *In The Frame – Integrated Education in Northern Ireland: The Implications of Expansion*. Coleraine: Centre for the Study of Conflict, 1999.
Gaffikin, F. and M. Morrissey, *Northern Ireland, the Thatcher Years*, London: Zed Books, 1990.
Galtung, J., *Peace By Peaceful Means*, Oslo: PRIO, 1996.
Gastrow, P., *Bargaining For Peace: South Africa and the National Peace Accord*. Washington: United States Institute for Peace, 1995.
Gidron, B., S. Katz, M. Meyer, Y. Hasenfeld, R. Schwartz, and J. Crane, 'Peace and Conflict Resolution Organisations in Three Protracted Conflicts: Structures, Resources and Ideology' in *Voluntas: International Journal of Voluntary and Non-Profit Organizations*. vol. 10, no. 4, 1999.
Hadfield, B., ed., *Northern Ireland: Politics and the Constitution*, Buckingham: Open University Press, 1993.
Hennnessey, T., *A History of Northern Ireland 1920–1996*, Dublin: Gill and Macmillan, 1997.
Hall, M., *Ulster's Protestant Working Class: A Community Exploration*, Belfast: Island Pamphlet 9. 1994.
Hermann, T., *Israeli Peace/Conflict Resolution NGOs 1967–1998, Final Report*. Tel Aviv: Tami Steinmetz Center for Peace Research, 1998. (unpublished)
Jay, R. and F. O'Boyle, *Poverty and Policy in the 1990s: The Role of the Voluntary Sector in Northern Ireland*, Belfast: Bryson House, 1988.
Knox, C., and Quirk, P., *Peace-Building in Northern Ireland, South Africa and Israel*. London: Macmillan, 2000.
Kreuger, R. A., *Focus Groups: A Practical Guide for Applied Research*, London: Sage Publications, 1988.
Lederach, J. P., *Building Peace: Sustainable Reconciliation in Divided Societies*. Washington DC: United States Institute of Peace Press, 1997.
Livingstone S. and J. Morison, *An Audit of Democracy in Northern Ireland*, Belfast: Fortnight Educational Trust, 1993.
Logue, K., *Anti-Sectarianism and the Voluntary and Community Sector*, Belfast: Community Relations Council, 1992.
Loughlin, J., *The Ulster Question Since 1945*. London: Macmillan, 1998.
McAuley, J. W., *The Politics of Identity*, Aldershot: Avebury, 1994.
McCrudden, C. 'Equality and the Good Friday Agreement' in Ruane, J., and J. Todd (eds), *After The Good Friday Agreement*. Dublin: University College Dublin Press, 1999, pp. 96–121.
McGarry, J. (ed.), *Northern Ireland and the Divided World*. Oxford: Oxford University Press, 2001.
Mallie, E., and D. McKittrick, *The Fight for Peace: The Secret Story Behind the Peace Process*. Belfast: Blackstaff Press, 1997.

Mitchell, P. and R. Wilford (eds) *Politics in Northern Ireland*. Oxford: Westview Press, 1999.

Montgomery, A., and A. Smith, *Values in Education in Northern Ireland*. Belfast: CCEA, 1997.

Morgan, V., S. Dunn, E. Cairns, and G. Fraser, *Breaking the Mould: The Role of Parents and Teachers in Integrated Schools in Northern Ireland*. Coleraine: Centre for the Study of Conflict, 1992.

Morgan, V. and G. Fraser *Women, Community and Organisations*, Centre for the Study of Conflict, University of Ulster, Coleraine, 1994.

Morrow, D., *The Churches and Inter-community Relationships*, Centre for the Study of Conflict, University of Ulster, Coleraine, 1991.

NICVA, *The State of the Sector – Northern Ireland Voluntary Sector Almanac*, Belfast: NICVA, 1996.

O'Connor, F., *In Search of A State: Catholics in Northern Ireland*. Belfast: Blackstaff Press, 1993.

O'Leary. B and J. McGarry, *The Politics of Antagonism: Understanding Northern Ireland*, London: The Athlone Press, 1993.

Oliver, Q., 'The Role of Non-profit Organisations in a Divided Society: The Case of Northern Ireland', in McCarthy K. D., V. A. Hodgkinson, and R. D. Sumariwalla, *The Non-profit Sector in the Global Community: Voices from Many Nations*, San Francisco: Jossey-Bass Publishers, 1992.

Oliver, Q., *Working for Yes: the story of the May 1998 referendum in Northern Ireland*. Belfast: The 'Yes' Campaign, 1998.

Ormsby, F. (ed.), *A Rage For Order: Poetry of the Northern Ireland Troubles*. Belfast: Blackstaff Press, 1992.

Payton, R. L., *Philanthropy: Voluntary Action for the Public Good*, London: Collier Macmillan, 1988.

Pollak, A., *A Citizen's Inquiry: The Opsahl Report on Northern Ireland*, Dublin: Lilliput Press, 1993.

Powell, F. and D. Guerin, *Civil Society and Social Policy*, Dublin: A. & A. Farmar, 1997.

Purdie, B., *Politics in the Streets: The Origins of the Civil Rights Movement in Northern Ireland*, Belfast: Blackstaff Press, 1990.

Putnam, R. D., 'Bowling Alone: America's Declining Social Capital', *Journal of Democracy*, 6, 1 January, 65–78.

Putnam, R. D., *Making Democracy Work: Civic Traditions in Modern Italy*, Princeton, NJ: Princeton University Press, 1993.

Ruane, J and J. Todd, eds, *After the Good Friday Agreement: Analysing Political Change in Northern Ireland*, University College Dublin Press, 1999.

Ruane, J. and J. Todd, *The Dynamics of Conflict in Northern Ireland*, Cambridge University Press, 1996.

Ruane, J., & J. Todd (eds), *After The Good Friday Agreement*. Dublin: University College Dublin Press, 1999.

Rupesinghe, K. (ed.), *Conflict Transformation*. London: Macmillan, 1995.

Ryan, S., 'Transforming Violent Intercommunal Conflict' in K. Rupesinghe (ed.) *Conflict Transformation*. London: Macmillan, 1995, pp. 223–65.

Salamon, L. M. and H. K. Anheier, 'The Non-profit Cross Nationally: Patterns and Types' in Saxon-Harrold, Susan K. E. et al., eds, *Researching the Voluntary Sector*, second edition, Charities Aid Foundation, 1994.

Smith, D. J. and G. Chambers, *Inequality in Northern Ireland*, Oxford: Clarendon Press, 1991.

Sugden, J. and S. Harvie, *Sport and Community in Northern Ireland*, Centre for the Study of Conflict, University of Ulster, Coleraine, 1993.

Weiss, T., 'Non-Governmental Organisations and Internal Conflict', in M. E. Brown (ed.), *The International Dimensions of Internal Conflict*. Massachusetts: MIT Press, 1996, pp. 435–60.

Whyte, J., *Interpreting Northern Ireland*, Oxford: Clarendon Press, 1990.

Index